DESIGNING THE GOOD HOME

DESIGNS OF

HUGH NEWELL JACOBSEN • BOHLIN CYWINSKI JACKSON • OBIE G. BOWMAN

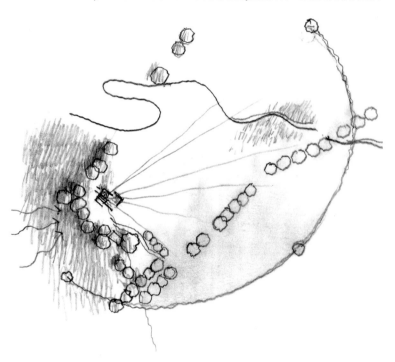

DESIGNING THE GOOD HOME

DESIGNS OF

HUGH NEWELL JACOBSEN • BOHLIN CYWINSKI JACKSON • OBIE G. BOWMAN

BY DENNIS WEDLICK

Written with Philip Langdon

HARPER DESIGN international

An imprint of HarperCollinsPublishers

Copyright © 2003 by Dennis Wedlick

First published in 2003 by
Harper Design International, an imprint of HarperCollins*Publishers*
10 East 53rd Street
New York, NY 10022-5299

Distributed throughout the world by
HarperCollins International
10 East 53rd Street
New York, NY 10022-5299
Fax: (212) 207-7654

ISBN: 0-06-008943-1
Library of Congress Control Number: 2003113949

Packaged by:
Grayson Publishing, LLC
James G. Trulove, Publisher
1250 28th Street NW
Washington, D.C. 20007
Tel: 202-337-1380
Fax: 202-337-1381
jtrulove@aol.com

Manufactured in Canada

First Printing, 2003

1 2 3 4 5 6 7 8 9 / 10 09 08 07 06 05 04 03

ACKNOWLEDGMENTS

Phil Landon and James Pittman collaborated with me on my first book The
Good Home *that featured the work of my own office. I am so pleased and
grateful that they were able to work with me again on* Designing The Good
Home; *without them I could not have realized the premise of this book.*

*I also would like to thank all those at the offices of Bohlin Cywinski Jackson,
Hugh Newell Jacobsen, Architect and Obie G.Bowman, Architect. Their contri-
butions and cooperation in producing this book made it possible to present the
finest work of today's residential architects. In my own office, I would like to
give a special acknowledgement to Chris Hunt as the liaison to all participants
of the book; his talent is greatly appreciated by all.*

HALF-TITLE PAGE Peter Bohlin's Gaffney Residence

TITLE PAGE Peter Bohlin's Goosewing Farm

FOREWORD

In his previous book, *The Good Home*, Dennis Wedlick set out to establish a common language we can all use to explain how and why successful houses work. Nearly all of us perceive when a house is flawed in some substantial way, but most of us lack the vision and voice to identify what's wrong. Dennis' first book helped us see and express what troubles us and what delights us about the houses we live in and visit. This book continues those admirable goals and adds a new purpose: to introduce us to a kinder, gentler Modernism we can all live with.

Today's user-friendly Modernism is the style we've been waiting for—where form doesn't just follow function, it embraces feeling, too. Looking to the past for inspiration is no longer verboten, so a house can look fresh and still feel familiar. Applied by a gifted architect, the style is original and evocative. It combines honest materials, simple forms, open floor plans, and an intimate connection to the land. It differs from previous incarnations of Modernism because the center is the natural world and the human realm rather than the machine age. Devoid of dogma, it allows for great flexibility of artistic expression and personal fulfillment for both the client and the architect.

There are few more fluent interpreters of this approach than Peter Bohlin, Hugh Newell Jacobsen, and Obie Bowman. Each has an aesthetic—a different sensibility through which he filters the world—but none has a specific agenda he's committed to applying. These architects aren't interested in simply imposing their vision on a client's lot. Instead, they're open to inspiration from any source, whether houses of the past, industrial buildings, elements of nature, or the half-remembered experience a client wishes to conjure. Answering the client's needs and doing justice to the site are their paramount concerns.

Existing houses and new production houses are all about decisions made with someone else in mind. Although a production builder may allow selection of some finishes and fixtures, the important floor planning and house siting have already been done. How the house lives is predetermined by a laundry list of generic demographic assumptions. The result is usually a strange amalgam of a semi-updated floor plan wrapped in a bygone architectural style. It's all half-measures, trapped between how we live now and how we used to live years ago. At first, the house may look pleasingly familiar, but it grows disturbing as the distortions and compromises sink in. This is often true of the remodeled older house as well, especially when an addition tacks onto an existing building with little or no change to the original house. Unfortunately, buyers may not detect these flaws until they've moved in and lived with the place awhile.

Our best opportunity for a truly satisfying house is to plan one from the ground up, using the site, our needs and desires, and the architect's technical and artistic expertise to steer the design. Rooted in genuine specifics and freed from stylistic constraints, the house can't help but feel personal—full of warmth and character.

Today's Modern house doesn't turn its back on the past, nor does it copy the pattern book verbatim. The result is dramatic and comfortable, timeless and fresh. Indeed, it makes a very good home.

—S. Claire Conroy is editor of *Residential Architect*.

TABLE OF CONTENTS

TABLE OF CONTENTS

DESIGNING THE GOOD HOME
THE MODERN THINKING THAT GUIDES TODAY'S PICTURESQUE HOUSES

A good home is not just a neutral vessel, blandly waiting for human activity to occur within its walls. A good home possesses character, or what might more precisely be called emotional resonance—the capacity to inspire thoughts and feelings in its occupants. Because I've been designing houses since the 1980s and because I've seen so many houses fail to connect emotionally with their owners, I make it my habit to try to figure out how houses stir the imagination. This book is part of my continuing search for guideposts that designers, builders, and prospective homeowners can use in their own effort to create satisfying homes.

Seen from a certain angle, the quest for emotional qualities in a dwelling verges on the mystical. Surely something magical happens when a house—which is an inanimate amalgam of wood, glass, metal, and an untold number of other substances—touches an individual's spirit. But identifying the sources of that magic and dissecting its workings are, to a large extent, a matter of intuition and experience, at least for me.

I think I've begun to make sense of what goes on, and in these pages I lay out a series of techniques you can use to design a house that will arouse feelings. I concentrate on houses that register on people emotionally and that are rooted in modern aesthetics and technology. These modern picturesque or modern romantic houses have the ability to affect us emotionally and at the same time suit contemporary ways of living. This dual focus—on feeling and on modern methods—is for me a critical element in how to design a good house.

What the past teaches us

Historically, feeling has been an important ingredient in American domestic architecture. In the seventeenth century, when the first permanent settlers from the British Isles and northern Europe arrived on this continent, they encountered a terrain that was unfamiliar and often inhospitable. The resources available in the new land were largely unknown. What they found in North America was so arduous and alien, so different from Europe, that the newcomers might as well have been colonizing the moon. In such a setting, shelter, even a rude, primitive one, was the first necessity. The settlers fashioned dwellings from whatever materials could be gathered within walking distance.

Like children using their imagination to build forts in back yards or in the woods, they assembled rustic dwellings to protect themselves from all that seemed strange or threatening—the extreme weather, the wild animals, and of course the natives already living in the vicinity. The colonists' first rudimentary creations were shoebox homes of stacked logs with pitched roofs, sometimes of earth—gathered together in a village pattern, their boundaries fortified when possible. As soon as possible, however, the primitive homes were added onto, or entirely new houses were built. The colonists wanted their homes to resemble the houses they had known in the Old World. The settlers had no interest whatsoever in emulating the Native Americans' building customs. Nor did they intend to invent new forms for the New World. Rather, the progress of North American house design throughout the next three hundred years consisted mainly in translating and adapting European antecedents to the houses that would be built here.

Although American builders looked to European models, their impulse was more romantic than historicist. They didn't so much copy Old World designs as invoke imagery that recalled certain places—such as villages in England, Germany, and the Netherlands. Early Americans built with the materials they found readily available, even if those materials had not commonly been used on the houses they were remembering.

ABOVE Some early American houses, like stone-walled Fort Klock, which Johannes Klock built in 1750 near St. Johnsville in New York's Mohawk Valley, were designed to ward off attacks. Because of their defensive intent and because glass was costly, houses often shut out the landscape, no matter how lush its beauty.

OPPOSITE A picturesque house and a barn that I designed in Kinderhook, in New York's Hudson Valley. Odd proportions, like those of a steep-pitched roof punctuated by a single dormer, often rouse people's feelings. The barn is modern in its bold shape, which makes a surprising contrast against the diminutive, almost quaint character of the house.

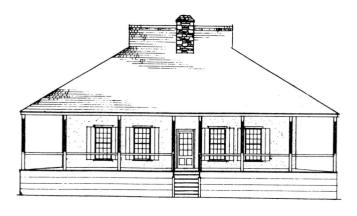

ABOVE The J.B. Valle house from about 1800 in Ste. Genevieve, Missouri, suggests an attempt to relate house to landscape. The raised porch beneath a high, hipped roof provides a sheltered outlook in the Mississippi River Valley, ruled at the time by France.

Americans erected houses predominantly of wood, even if the inspirations for the designs were European dwellings of masonry. Some wooden eighteenth-century structures became known as Dutch colonials despite the fact that they conveyed impressions of Dutch houses that had been built of stone.

Even when American homes used the same materials as those on the other side of the Atlantic, such as stone or brick, they were hardly ever identical to the European originals. Americans adapted European imagery and styles to new conditions, different landscapes. In the nineteenth century, Italianate and Queen Anne cottages were built on beaches or on oceanfront cliffs in styles that recalled homes in the Italian countryside or in English suburbs.

For Americans, literal reproductions of houses from the old country could rarely suit the lifestyles of a new industrious and democratic society. The mansions of the upper class overseas were generally considered too ostentatious for capitalist tycoons in the United States, even if the American versions did turn out to be quite elaborate. The cottages of Europe's lower class also did not lend themselves to copying—for an opposite reason: they were too inferior to house the New World's working class. Old homes in Europe's countryside had been designed without comfort-giving technologies such as central heating and indoor plumbing, and they had used glass sparingly—partly because it was terribly costly and partly because historic European architecture had sought to keep the world out. That defensive posture continued in some American houses, such as dwellings in the 1700s in New York's Mohawk Valley that were called "forts" because they were designed to ward off attacks by French and Indians. But as Hugh Newell Jacobsen pointed out to me, American architecture quickly shifted to a different path, and houses in the New World stopped being built for defense. American architects displayed an eagerness to let in the sun, the landscape, and the neighbors.

I believe that this embrace of the charm of European homes—even while avoiding the negatives associated with European life—is what makes American homes, and other colonial architecture throughout the world, so romantic and alluring. Today what's fascinating about American house design is that it draws imagery and sentiment from one world and mixes it with technology and methods from another. A number of contemporary architects, myself included, are inspired by the dynamics of this modern romantic sensibility. This approach is well suited to the many people who vow to build their own homes because their vision of the ideal home is not shared by "production home-builders" (the building industry's term for tract-home builders). Like the Americans of long ago, many people are torn between two worlds: one that arouses the feelings associated with a good home and one dictated by basic needs, location, and finances. In my experience, many clients crave a home that will satisfy complex aspirations—that will offer surprises and gratifying sensations while also being modern and functional.

Modern picturesque architects

Homeowners-to-be often seek out architects whose work resonates with those aspirations. I too have sought out such architects for inspiration. I have chosen three of them to be the subject of this book: Hugh Newell Jacobsen, Peter Bohlin, and Obie Bowman. The three have much in common, yet they produce work that is remarkably divergent. That should not be surprising, since these are architects who dare to test new recipes for designing a good home and who take a free-spirited approach to their work. What they share is a love of life and landscape, a passion about modern construction technologies, and a penchant for the familiar. Their work is not historicist, but it is picturesque. It is evocative—suggestive of ingrained associations—even as it is new. These designers are modern romantics—architects adept at producing contemporary houses that arouse emotion, that have soul.

The three I've selected invent new forms, but not for the sake of inventing new forms. They devise interesting shapes to engage the viewers' and inhabitants' feelings, just as romantic designers have done for generations. Their houses are wondrously unique, yet not alien. They

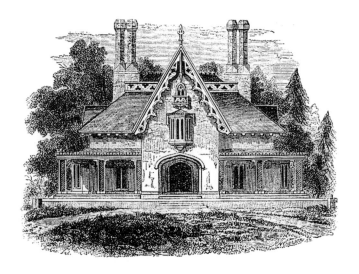

TOP When Andrew Jackson Downing published this "cottage-villa in the rural Gothic style" in 1850, he drew attention to its picturesque qualities: "The high pointed gable of the central and highest part of this design has a bold and spirited effect, which would be out of keeping with the cottage-like modesty of the drooping, hipped roof, were it not for the equally bold manner in which the chimney-tops spring upwards."

BOTTOM A modern house by Hugh Newell Jacobsen looks much simpler, yet its upward-thrusting shapes and a few well-chosen details, such as vertical battens, evoke the feeling of nineteenth-century Gothic Revival.

remind visitors of something familiar, whether it's a saltbox house that's common in their neighborhood or an old farm shed that they saw on a trip across the Midwest, or something they cannot quite put their finger on. Jacobsen builds homes, mainly in the eastern U.S. and Canada, whose profiles in the bright sunlight suggest the skyline of a village. Bohlin has used barn-like shapes for homes in various parts of America, and has designed provocative houses whose shapes bring to mind assemblies of garden walls and lean-tos. Bowman has created houses on the Pacific coast whose profiles look as if they might first have been seen by pioneers heading west in a wagon train. Some houses by Bowman are bold in design, but are wedged into the landscape so as not to intrude upon the context or the neighbors.

These three architects never tire of the art and craft of home-building. They push humble, affordable materials into mimicking the much more costly substances of which castles and monuments are made. Every detail from the nosing on a stair tread to the flashing of a chimney is for Jacobsen, Bohlin, and Bowman another opportunity to pursue a better way of building. Like old cobblers, they fret about whether their houses are comfortable to live in and whether they are built well enough to last. Their concern with how people respond is what makes these designers romantic and sets them apart from architects who detail with only the sculptural quality of construction, rather than feeling, in mind. I had the pleasure of seeing first-hand that their obsession with seeking and applying the newest technologies is not aimed at being avant-garde but at being sure they are producing good homes.

Each of the three adapts to the site, whether on the shore of an ocean, at the edge of a precipice, or in the middle of a farmer's field. All of them manipulate the

ABOVE LEFT The intricate yet powerful structure of an old barn that was framed in a German tradition that employs complex interior bents, at Springton Manor in Chester County, Pennsylvania.

LEFT A modern house by Peter Bohlin in Ontario, Canada, captures the flavor of the barn, only better, because ample sunlight plays across the timbers.

landscape's attributes in conjunction with the home's layout, hiding a view from the visitor until just the right moment. They meticulously fit the home to the site and wrench out every possible attribute the location can offer. These are architects who know that a single tree can be a wonderful landscape. They can make the most of exceedingly humble properties as well as magnificent ones.

Their buildings are not shelters whose sole purpose is to contain life. They are homes that let life in, let nature in. The three do not build "glass houses"; they frame nature with windows. The patterns of the glass transform views into portraits that are capable of revealing nature's complexity. They harness the sun so that it brightens corners, casts deep shadows, remains neutral when it ought to, and makes the homes richer and more complex. There is no doubt, though, that each of the architects in this book is his own person. Each of these architects has a flair for the picturesque.

The meaning of "picturesque" design

I use the word "picturesque" differently than most people do. Today picturesque is often taken to mean "pretty"—or pretty with an overlay of quaintness. I instead use the term the way art historians do—to refer to an aesthetic approach that emphasizes irregular and unexpected features that catch people's attention and engage their interest. That was the sense of picturesque that prevailed among many Americans in the middle of the nineteenth century, when architect Alexander Jackson Davis and landscape designer Andrew Jackson Downing ranked among the nation's most prominent tastemakers. Davis and Downing disliked the strictness of the Greek Revival; they rejected houses modeled on temples from the classical world, and they insisted that American houses should aim for a more informal and expressive character. In *The Architecture of Country Houses*, Downing wrote that domestic architecture "should exhibit more of the freedom and play of feeling of every-day life." In my first book, *The Good Home: Interiors and Exteriors*, I made the case that houses today should be designed in a picturesque manner, and presented several

TOP A house by Obie Bowman on the Oregon coast allows its occupants to feel as if they're outside, even while fully sheltered from the elements. This quest to bring the outdoors in is a strong theme of modern residential design.

BOTTOM Richard Neutra's VDL Research House, built in California in 1932, is a modern house that achieved the same aim at a time when great sheets of glass were uncommon.

TOP *The ground extends onto the roof of a Bowman house, folding it into the landscape. In effect, the house burrows into the earth—one way of relating a home to its setting.*

BOTTOM *Long ago, as Eric Sloane sketched in* American Barns and Covered Bridges, *structures in farm country were sometimes built with their long slope oriented to the north, obtaining a measure of protection against cold winter winds. A design of this kind imparts a strong sense of shelter.*

homes of my own design as examples.

By the 1840s and 1850s, thanks to Davis and Downing, the Picturesque Movement had started to influence American houses. The movement encompassed a number of styles, including Stick Style, Queen Anne, and—the mode that architectural historian Vincent Scully identified as a high point of American domestic design—the relaxed and relaxing Shingle Style. A picturesque house is not shy about incorporating irregularity and expressiveness or about arousing sentiment. The designer may exaggerate the shape and prominence of the roof, give windows unusual dimensions, or prolong the experience of entering the house. A room may rise surprisingly high, to generate a sense of expansiveness, or its walls may slope down, to create a cozy, enveloping refuge. Picturesque houses allow experimentation and departures from the norm. It is these departures, exaggerations, surprises, and mysteries that invest a house with feeling and give it soul. The picturesque is a form of romanticism, an approach that prizes emotion and imagination. So in this book I sometimes call these three "picturesque architects" and at other times call them "modern romantics." They brilliantly combine romantic traits and modern methods.

When I first proposed presenting the work of these three architects, the reaction was always the same: Why Hugh Newell Jacobsen, and who is Obie Bowman? Peter Bohlin was the only identifiable modern romantic of the bunch. When I met Peter at his home in Waverly, Pennsylvania, he was as confident as I that he would belong in any book on picturesque homes. Architects have a great fear of being misinterpreted (because it happens so often), and Peter Bohlin's initial concern was that I would show only his projects that had cottage-like profiles. Peter is a renowned designer, but many of his most published projects have traditional attributes: gable roofs, wood-frame construction, and common house parts such as columns, double-hung windows, and porches. The traditional projects have the virtue of being the most affordable of his designs; the cost is naturally higher for nontraditional buildings made entirely of custom-made components. Despite the quality of the work he's done in a relatively traditional vein, Peter didn't want readers to get a skewed view, one that would ignore his more nontraditional designs.

This book therefore features diverse projects of Peter's firm, Bohlin Cywinski Jackson. Some of the houses shown are relatively simple, with fairly traditional profiles, whereas others are more complex, exhibiting modernist elements such as flat roofs. Regardless of the budget or the character, the genesis of a Bohlin house does not vary. Peter starts, as each of these architects does, by intensely studying the property's potential to take advantage of natural features: sunlight, vegetation, and views, to name a few. The next step is to work out a simple geometrical organization of the house on its land. What that generally means is that Peter takes the plan of the house—which is based on the size and functions required by the homeowner—and incorporates it into a diagram of lines and rectangles showing where the views are, how people approach the house, how large the parking area or the patios should be, and where any special landscape features should be situated. The lines and rectangles are laid down according to an academic set of proportions. The goal, though, is not academic. Peter wants the house to please the homeowner with its beauty, and he wants the house to be well suited to its landscape.

Inside and out, Peter's houses exude warmth that transcends the nature of their materials. Why some of his houses feel warm is obvious—he's been known to line a home's interior with wood on nearly every surface. A preferred wood for Peter is clear Douglas fir finished with satin polyurethane that glows, like a flame, with the littlest bit of light. Other homes are constructed with rough concrete, metal connections, and sheetmetal sheathing, industrial materials all, yet as Peter assembles and details them, they take on the same warmth as their wood counterparts. The best way to describe how he accomplishes this is to refer to agricultural buildings. Farmers have rarely been shy about using crude or industrial materials to build the structures they need, such as grain silos, milking barns, and storage sheds. As these structures have aged, they have blended into the

TOP A house by Jacobsen practically floats above its landscape, creating a setting where people can feel immersed in nature.

BOTTOM Jacobsen's house strikingly recalls the tent platforms that vacationers often used in the late nineteenth century, when summer accommodations like these on Upper St. Regis Lake in the Adirondacks were rudimentary. A house can respect nature by making a purposefully light imprint on the land.

TOP A California design by Bowman shows how a private, protected outdoor space can add to a house's allure.

BOTTOM Philip Johnson's Ash Street house in Cambridge, Massachusetts, in 1942, also featured a protected outdoor space—on view from inside the home.

agricultural landscape, coming to look as natural as the crops and the livestock. Peter uses these same materials in ways that recall their practical and unpretentious application by farmers. They initially appear to have been chosen mostly just to get the job done, but the final result is enchanting.

No one could imagine Hugh Newell Jacobsen employing the warm palette of Peter Bohlin, which is why bringing these two architects together into one book surprised many of the people I spoke with. The fact is, both Jacobsen and Bohlin restrict themselves to a very limited palette in order to create beautiful houses; the palettes are simply different. Where Bohlin covers floors, walls, and ceilings with Douglas fir, Jacobsen makes all the surfaces white. That difference has made an impact on how the two architects are regarded. Being known for all-wood homes has made Bohlin touchy about not being thought of as a modernist. Being known as a master of all-white homes has made Jacobsen sensitive to being seen *only* as a modernist. When I spoke with Jacobsen, he complained about potential clients who avoid him because they think he is too much of a modernist.

In truth, few designers have a more romantic orientation than Jacobsen. His homes may be all-American in shape—perfect profiles of gable-roofed New England houses are part of his repertoire—yet he straddles two worlds, finishing those traditionally shaped homes with white-painted brick and sheets of glass: materials and details more often associated with modern office buildings. Whereas photographs of Bohlin's interiors easily exude warmth, presentations of Jacobsen's struggle to avoid appearing cold. "Warm and cozy" is a maternal attribute possessing undeniable appeal, but we should recognize that bright, airy, and clean are equally sensual attributes. Jacobsen designs homes that are meant to be loved for a lifetime, and he makes a point of telling his clients so. Many people feel at peace in a comfortable mess—a fact sometimes used in arguments against the purity of Modern design—but just as many, if not more, find peace in tidiness, orderliness, and Puritan principles, essential parts of Jacobsen's lasting appeal.

Jacobsen designs homes to be successful in their efficient use of space, in their spareness and avoidance of frivolous details, and in their no-nonsense relationship to the landscape. The effect is nevertheless romantic because efficiency, in Jacobsen's hands, achieves the character of poetry.

When Jacobsen chooses the site for a house, he finds the sweet spot that will make a striking impression on visitors and that will allow the landscape to change constantly as the visitors take each step toward it or around it. Jacobsen's houses do not need the assistance of a screen of foliage or the curve of a hill to make them vigorous. The shape and the layout of the house are dynamic in themselves. The house's profile may consist not of a single, simple gable form, or of the even simpler flat roof form, but of multiple volumes assembled like cards—one lapped over another, partly concealing and partly revealing the next. These are then arranged into V-configurations or into courtyards or rambling compounds, depending on the light, the topography, or the views. There is no dogmatic reason for laying out a house this way. Jacobsen simply knows that a design of this sort will be satisfying to live in and that with this layout, the house will make the best of the land it sits on. Jacobsen's compound layouts serve more than one purpose; they enliven the approach to the house, dramatize movement through the interior, and enhance ordinary experiences such as sitting at the dining room table—all good picturesque reasons for designing in this fashion.

Then there is Obie Bowman. Visiting Bowman at his office, you are not surprised that few people have heard of him. Nestled into beautiful countryside in northern California (where wealthy families start vineyards for the fun of it) lies a aluminum Airstream trailer small enough to be pulled by a Volkswagen Beetle. This is the main office of Obie Bowman Architects. All the bravado of Peter Bohlin and Hugh Newell Jacobsen combined would not be enough antimatter to negate the modesty of Obie Bowman. Yet just like those two, Bowman has the skills and the power to bring nature to its knees. The Pacific coast, Bowman territory, is far

TOP A roof trellis creates a lacy shadow pattern on the natural-toned wall of a Bowman house. Materials—and their appearance in natural and artificial lighting and under different atmospheric conditions—give a house part of its allure.

BOTTOM A similar sense of extending outward and attention to the intrinsic character of materials distinguish the Adelaide M. Tichenor house that the influential Pasadena firm Greene & Greene designed in 1905.

TOP Restraint can be a powerful aesthetic, linking a new house to the character of dwellings built two or more centuries ago, as demonstrated by Jacobsen's Greene residence on Chesapeake Bay.

BOTTOM At a Shaker settlement near Lexington, Kentucky, simplicity and restraint announce themselves through straightforward shapes, more wall than window, and a near-absence of decoration. Some houses achieve expressiveness through purity and discipline.

more fierce than places like the shores of Virginia where Jacobsen's clients have settled down in his troupe of colonial shapes. In settings where the wind refuses to let trees grow taller than flag poles, Bowman's structures wedge themselves underneath the landscape's skin. Permanently embedded, they are impossible to move.

The forms Bowman uses are not entirely unfamiliar, and they blend remarkably into the scenery. From the outside, they appear reclusive. A Bowman design may be a courtyard house on the coast, or a three-story dwelling with a tiny footprint squeezed between the trees in a forest, or an earth-bermed house with ground cover growing up and over the roof. Visitors must find their way to the front door, yet they are subtly led by what seems to be some mystical force. This is an aspect of good picturesque design. Like the view to the house itself, the view to the ocean, the distant hills, or just to the evening sky is held back, then revealed, then taken away again, to give the lucky homeowners more pleasure than any ordinary home would render. The exterior is visually forceful yet it seems less rigid or organized than Bohlin's or Jacobsen's designs, giving Bowman houses a deceptively hodge-podge composition.

All three of these architects inject a bit of levity into the mix. Jacobsen's prim and proper clapboard houses have big holes cut into them. Bohlin's houses have giant window boxes globbed on like big warts. Bowman leans absurdly large posts against a house; the house would cave in from the weight if it weren't for the hidden structure. The textures, colors, and scale of the building parts that make up the exterior may seem organic, but they're actually a bit affected, considering their location. For example, a closer look at the hefty column of tree trunk used to frame the entry to a Bowman house would reveal that neither is it structurally essential nor is it cut from a tree that could be found on that land. As with all romantic architects, the possibility of creating a delightful or humorous composition is sometimes the only reason Bowman needs to add one more bracket or beam to a façade.

On the interiors, ordinary house-building becomes extraordinary, because nothing is taken for granted.

Waste not, want not is the best way to describe Bowman's interior wall construction. What homeowner could not use another set of shelves for books, trophies, or family photos? Wherever possible, Bowman exposes the wood members that hold up interior walls, and he assembles them into a beautiful matrix of cubbyholes. Rooms are positioned up and down, here and there, as if they had built on uneven ground so that there is a natural flow throughout the house. Bowman uses inventive construction techniques to make fantastic interior spaces that the child in everyone would love. The families that inhabit them enjoy enchanting, cave-like corners in seemingly impossible places. Some Bowman houses have fully suspended platforms large enough for an entire master bedroom, even if the home is tiny.

All three are master architects. One purpose of this book is to demystify what makes them astonishing, so that their work can be admired more widely. My other purpose is to present modern homes that embody feelings, expression, and a love of nature. It is important to see these architects together, for it is through comparison that their common threads—their approach to the landscape and construction technologies, and their use of memorable forms—are revealed. This is the only way to recognize the picturesque techniques and principles that are the foundations of their practice, since they take many different final forms. That says a great deal about the potential of the picturesque. What I have tried to illustrate here is an approach that allows the individual homeowner and the architect to invent a completely unique residence without abandoning all those things that are sentimental, poetic, and familiar.

TOP The bold shape terminating a hallway and the elimination of unnecessary details at a nineteenth-century Shaker village in South Union, Kentucky, are almost modern in feeling.

BOTTOM The shape of the ceiling gives the master bedroom its character in this house of my design in Dutchess County, New York. Shapes are sometimes most powerful when stripped to their essence.

PART I
MODERN TECHNIQUES

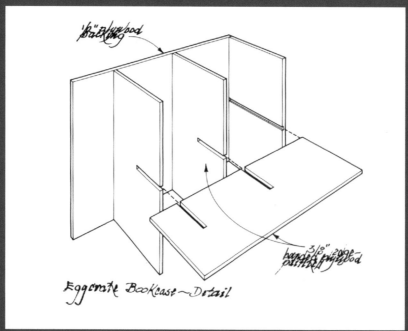

Hugh Newell Jacobsen's Egg crate bookshelf.

Peple generally think of modern houses as having little trim or ornamentation, lots of glass, and flat roofs whose proportions are exaggerated—sometimes extremely long, sometimes dramatically cantilevered, and sometimes exactly the opposite: hardly visible at all. The image of the modern house took root some seven decades ago, and although the avant-garde gave up the prohibition on sloped roofs more than half a century ago, the sense of what is "modern" has remained fairly consistent.

In contrast to modern houses, traditional houses are generally thought to have old-fashioned windows—either double-hung or casement—with multiple panes of glass. Instead of flat roofs, traditional houses tend to have gable or hip roofs, and on the interior and exterior, they often display classically-inspired trim and ornamentation. Many architects once expected that modern houses, which appeared on the scene around the dawn of the twentieth century, would eventually replace all the older styles of dwellings everywhere. And yet the revolution stalled. Modern design made an enormous impact on offices and other workplaces, but it never achieved its goal for the domestic side of life. In the eastern portions of the United States, you need only visit a few new residential developments to see that the traditional styles have remained firmly established. In the Northeast, where I live, the center-hall colonial remains the single most popular form of house, generations after the passing of Wright, Le Corbusier, and other heralds of new ways of designing.

When so much of life has changed, when four or five generations have passed since Americans traded in horse and buggy for a vehicle with a gasoline-powered engine, why hasn't the appearance of the modern house ever really caught on? One reason may be that many people find modern houses cold and alienating. A house needs to resonate with people's emotions if it is to be considered a home. Some people, it's true, get a thrill from the rigor and the other attributes of modern homes. They love their shapes, which can be unusual (they don't have to resemble a cube). Admirers of modernism tend to like industrial materials, and are happy at the absence of details that have already been used millions of times. These same attributes strike other people as harsh or downright intimidating. Novel or unfamiliar forms drive many people away, especially when the house's colors, textures, and finishes are also severe or out of the ordinary.

In my view, the techniques and details of good modern design can achieve tremendous beauty. When a modern approach is rendered in warm materials and is shaped into a romantic composition, the results can be more endearing than is the case with many traditional houses. A modern simple column made of exposed cedar can, in a woodland setting, be far more pleasing than a porch post designed in a classical style or one that's been ornately painted to mimic those of historical houses.

The architects whose work is presented here—Peter Bohlin, Hugh Newell Jacobsen, and Obie Bowman—all build modern houses employing modern details and modern techniques. The houses they create may not look nearly as familiar as a center-hall colonial, but they are not cold or alienating. These houses are built of wood and other materials found in their regions. They appear so natural in their settings that it is often difficult to tell when the houses were constructed, even though each is clearly modern in style. These houses have interiors that may be warm or cool, but are always sensual. The living quarters of these houses are filled with natural light, refreshed by cool breezes, and blessed with fantastic views, thanks to the modern use of glass and the decision to use open floor plans. Their unusual shapes and dramatic roofs give these houses a unique character, one not available in a traditional dwelling. Consequently, they can express something about their homeowners or their location and the inspiration that brought them into being. A traditional house can be tweaked, with a change of layout, to suit the site or the occupant's lifestyle better, but it cannot be as imaginative, as wholly creative, as a modern house can be. These architects whose work I examine in the pages that follow create houses that have the comfort and warmth of traditional houses, but that deliver the sometimes breathtaking advantages of modern design.

Modern houses are built with exciting shapes, with interiors that are not ornate, and with ample areas of glass. They wield dramatic assemblies of volumes; in some instances the volumes themselves are not out of the ordinary, but they are always bold. Detailing of the interiors spans the entire spectrum from highly traditional moldings to little or no trim, yet all of these houses emphasize a restrained palette; they are purposely limited in color and texture. They are built with a modern appreciation for the artistic qualities inherent in construction—the structure, joinery, and detailing not only hold the building together; they serve as compelling decoration. The ample expanses of glass typically are organized into a grid pattern of window panes, a signal of their modernity. The way the glass is arranged, proportioned, and divided gives the interior its comfortable atmosphere and enhances the view of the outdoors, at the same time preventing the occupants from feeling overly exposed. Properly handled, modern techniques are not cold or alienating; they are bold, artistic, and sensual.

BOLD SHAPES

odern houses shy away from traditional embellishments. Instead they rely on bold shapes to make an impression. The more dramatic the shape, the more expressive the design is likely to be. A greatly simplified version of a traditional house shape can, for instance, make a strong visual impact and yet convey associations with the past. In New England, one possibility would be to use the shape of a colonial-era saltbox, without any of its historical trappings. Even when stripped of old-fashioned details such as small, multiple-pane windows, the saltbox form powerfully communicates a sense of "home" and affinity with its region.

The design of a modern home may be composed of a number of minimalist shapes. The bold shapes could be drawn from residential architecture, but they don't have to be. They might be fantastic, almost surreal; in some instances, they appear to defy gravity or to be unrelated to the house's construction system. Bold shapes can make for a house with a unique relationship to the landscape. Dramatic shapes have the ability to float over their adjacencies; a house with a large roof and giant overhangs can appear to hover above the first floor and the landscape. A crisply shaped house may seem to sit lightly on the land, looking as if it could easily be removed.

Boldness may also be achieved by giving a traditionally detailed house a remarkably steep roof or an oddly shaped footprint. You might enlarge the scale of traditional details, for instance employing an oversized chimney or extra-large dormers. The strong shapes used in a home's exterior and interior are often symbols that can relate to the house's setting. A towering chimney may remind you of nearby trees or of the history of the region. Dormers may have shapes that are exaggerated versions of a local tradition. They may also reflect the predilections of the owners for a particular profile, such as that of a barn. The modern romantic will balance the composition to consist of just a few strong shapes so that the house is expressive without being too confusing or showy.

LEFT A modern house in Adirondack style practically jumps out toward those who walk up the stone entry path. Despite being covered in rustic materials, the shape is bold—and made still more emphatic by being supported on a pair of stout logs. It has a gutsy quality.

ABOVE The paring back of overhangs almost to the point of disappearance allows the irregular wall profiles to stand out. The boldness is accentuated by the angles and asymmetry and by limiting the exterior to one material.

LEFT Asymmetry abounds in this simple building. The door is off-center, with a window on one side but not on the other. The fieldstone wall at the left is not closely balanced by the sloping wood wall at the right. The roof flaunts its irregular composition. All these elements create a bold appearance for what might otherwise have been a humble, old-fashioned-looking shed.

ABOVE Deep overhangs and thin posts with butt-jointed glass at the corner make the roof shape bold.

BELOW A busy composition of jutting triangles, a big, straight-up chimney, and a prominent bay window makes a forceful impression. All the visual commotion engenders assertiveness.

RIGHT A strong, angular profile gains further intensity from the rugged log supports.

ABOVE An incomplete stone wall looking like a ruin, and a trellis above part of it, make eye-catching forms in the landscape for a bold impression. Other shapes, such as the garage, can remain undemonstrative when elements in the foreground seize the viewer's attention.

ABOVE Breaking a big house into a series of simple, repeating volumes produces a powerful and confident composition. The repeating trellis form magnifies the house's potency.

FOLLOWING PAGES The shape of each pavilion is reduced to the fewest and sharpest strokes and then repeated for stunning effect.

RESTRAINED PALETTE

Simplicity is a trademark of the good modern home. One way of achieving simplicity on the interior and exterior—while achieving expressiveness in the home's details, textures, and compositions—is to limit variation in the house's materials and colors. The restrained palette ties everything together and generates simplicity. For example, let's suppose you were eager to surround yourself with natural materials and you wanted a certain eclectic touch, yet you also wanted your home to be modern. One way to achieve this on the interior would be with smooth wide-plank floors, walls made of knotty beadboard, ceilings edged with carved crown moldings, and giant grid-pattern windows made of yellow pine. Such an interior would abound with wood, and it would be eclectic in its aesthetics—crown moldings are more formal than either the plank floors or the knotty walls—yet the uniformity of materials and color would give the house a distinctly contemporary character. A house may have many features and details, but if they are monochromatic, it will appear as minimalist and modern as a house whose features and details are few.

Limiting the palette on the exterior accomplishes a number of objectives for the modern romantic. Without the distraction of multiple colors or finishes, the simple and powerful shapes of the house stand out. You can indulge in mixing contrasting kinds of details if you keep them all within a narrow spectrum of color and materials.

Traditional details might be chosen to express the heritage of the region or the personal taste of the homeowner and blended with modern details into a pleasing, consistent ensemble.

A home is often more harmonious with the landscape when the exterior adheres to a limited palette. The colors can be carefully chosen to match those of the natural features of the property. Materials can be selected according to what could be found in the surrounding landscape, such as local woods and stones. A colorful, showy house might compete with the views, the countryside, or neighboring buildings, whereas a good design that sticks to a simple palette would tend to fit in.

LEFT The use of just one material, redwood, unites a rambling, informal composition and creates an air of simplicity. Because each piece of wood has a subtly different color and grain and weathers unpredictably, the restrained palette is not dull—it's alluring.

ABOVE Humble, unshowy materials—cedar shakes covering the walls and roofs—let the crisply composed volumes of the house read strongly and make a modern impression.

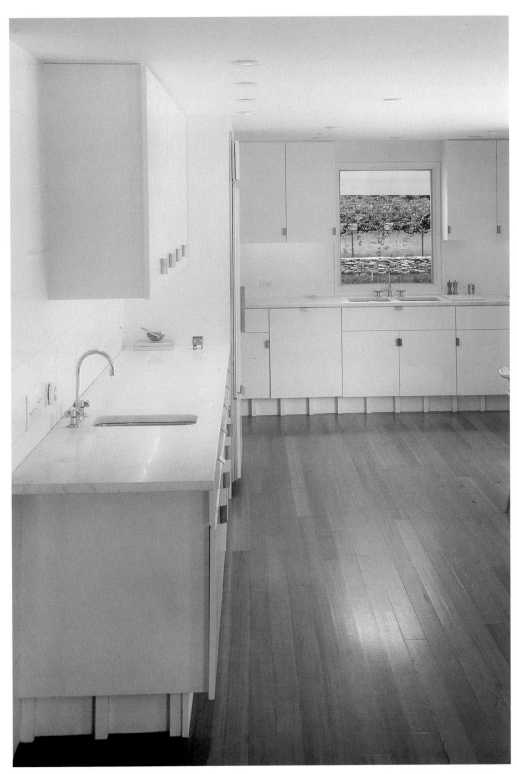

LEFT With the wall, the door, and the muntins of the large window painted white and with the redwood deck stained a soft gray, all that's needed to give this exterior some punch is a touch of another color—green trim around a tiny window.

ABOVE The floor of recycled antique heart pine and the other surfaces of white create a restrained aesthetic, so the splash of color of the view through the window stands out, the way a beautiful painting on a monochromatic wall would grab attention.

ABOVE A humble material such as plywood can achieve a rich, elegant look when one material is used throughout. Keeping everything a single color or tone makes a small space more aggressive and, conversely, makes a large space cozier. The smallest bit of light, in the gable window, becomes impressive when the palette is limited.

LEFT By using a single material—wood—in a single color, this interior's glowing floor, walls, and ceiling manifest a modern flair. The orange-toned wood looks as if it generates more warmth than the fireplace does. Because the old-fashioned barn doors conform to the monochromatic color palette, they do not undercut the modern effect.

ABOVE *The impact of natural light is intensified when the interior is restricted to wood in a narrow color range. With few colors to compete for attention, the light becomes soft and soothing—refuting the notion that modern design is necessarily cold.*

ABOVE Light has a powerful effect when the surfaces it strikes are limited to white painted wood and natural strip flooring. The light becomes intense and sensual.

ABOVE Two tones, wood and white, dramatize this room's contemporary character when sunlight pours in. The restrained use of color allows furnishings to take the foreground.

ABOVE Keeping the walls white calls attention to the texture of the brick and mortar and focuses attention on the jaggedness of the profile. In the sunlight, the walls become a perfect canvas for the trees' shadows, creating a chiaroscuro effect.

GRIDS OF GLASS

Owners of modern homes delight in patterns. They admire designs that repeat again and again, such as plaids, stripes, and grids. The patterns can produce a variety of effects, from calming to unnerving. One popular modern pattern is the grid, in which each unit is a rectangle of identical size. This pattern is supremely restful, so easy on the eyes that it can practically disappear even while it generates a calming sense of order and control.

Modern windows are often divided into grids of glass through the use of muntins. Long ago muntins were a necessity, since the only sizes in which glass could be produced at reasonable cost were tiny. For decades, however, manufacturers have been able to produce glass in large dimensions, so muntins have to a great extent become something chosen for aesthetic reasons rather than an essential element of window construction. In fact, it's now less costly to make a single pane measuring, say, four feet square than to assemble many small panes into a window of that size. Modern architects frequently divide windows into patterns composed of smaller pieces of glass because they want to layer a pattern over the openings in the wall. The muntins may be nothing but a decorative appliqué.

Window grid patterns do triple duty. First, they add to a house's walls a proportioning feature that can be a pleasing, recurring motif. The house may have windows that are all in similar sizes and shapes, or it may have a varied assortment of windows, but all divided into panes of one size. Another alternative is for the house to have a few unusually sized or shaped windows, serving as eye-catching features. Second, the grid patterns add a design feature to a room's interior. A large window meticulously divided into a grid of glass can be a focal point, just as a stained glass window would be. Finally, a grid of glass can enhance enjoyment of a landscape by splitting the view into a series of framed scenes. And when no one piece of glass could be built large enough to take in the whole view, a. grid of windows can capture the panorama.

ABOVE Grids of glass above give an almost monumental character to this house. The effect is created with assemblies of inexpensive glass doors.

LEFT A division of a large window into pieces of equal size is a signature of modernists. It frames a series of small scenes within the overall view and creates an orderly pattern.

LEFT The industrial sash brings the outside in. The glass, with its lacy pattern, becomes a surface to be savored, not just a void. The glass grid steps down toward a sunken seating area in the corner.

TOP RIGHT Equal division of window panes is associated with modernists, but in some instances it could just as easily be part of a traditional house.

BOTTOM RIGHT Thin muntins tend to give a window a modern feeling.

PRECEDING PAGES A continuous grid spreads across several otherwise ordinary windows, generating a compelling modern quality for the interior of a rustic house. An expansive grid can create an aesthetic that is both relaxing and controlled.

ABOVE Rustic posts and beams standing free of the walls dramatize and decorate the interior beautifully. The structure adds visual interest while it adds a layer to the interior.

EXPOSED STRUCTURE

The classic modern home is known for its lack of decorative touches: the absence of crown moldings at the ceiling, the elimination of elaborate trim around windows or doors, and so on. This is not to say that those who design modern houses are uninterested in making things pleasing to the eye. Far from it. They recognize that the most beautiful aspect of the modern home may be the structure itself. The structure, when well designed and well executed, can be breathtaking. The interior is often designed so that the construction is exposed rather than concealed within the layers of the walls or hidden above the ceilings. Exposed structural parts such as beams and posts do not have decorative classical details added to them or carved into them, but they are detailed to be attractive to look at and to add character to the entire interior.

The modernist is often obsessed with the way the house is put together. After all, the origins of modernism lie in new construction technologies such as reinforced concrete, steel beams, and structural glass. The classic modernist is known for employing a universal approach to construction, whether the construction of a house or the construction of an airplane hanger.

Modernists, however, have become less dogmatic over the years, and there is now considerable diversity in the approaches they take. The architects whose work is presented here share a passion for beautiful and innovative construction, but they employ much humbler materials, such as wood and masonry. For most of their houses, they use methods of building that any skillful carpenter can execute. The results, though far less industrial than those associated with orthodox modernists, are no less impressive and are more suitable to the creation of comfortable homes in the countryside. Visible structure may be as rough-hewn as logs or it may be smooth and regular. It may consist almost entirely of wood, or it may use metal or other materials. The exposed structure not only adds drama to the interiors, but also helps establish the character of the home or express the nature of the surrounding landscape.

ABOVE A more restrained pattern of large and smaller beams gives a fascinating look to a pitched ceiling.

ABOVE A lacy trellis creates a focal point and, because of its shadow pattern, adds interest to the wall below it. The slotted structure of the wall also generates aesthetic interest on its own.

RIGHT Conspicuous brackets and posts make a modern house more flamboyant. The exposed metal straps exude a tough decorative quality.

ABOVE A wooden girder with its reinforcing diagonal bracing is a strong focal point in this interior, where the structure is used for dramatic purposes.

LEFT A straightforward layering of beams and joists gives modern character to an open interior. Even the built-ins reflect attention to how things are put together and contribute to the house's personality.

ABOVE The contrast between the log wall and the industrial truss system animates this interior. Timber posts and laminated wood beams complete the structural ensemble. Structure can be poetic.

ABOVE Oversized structural members in a very small house crown the upper part of the interior. Modern industrial materials and structure can energize a house.

ABOVE Traditional stick-frame construction, exposed in a renovation, creates a screen between two spaces.

RIGHT PHOTOS An unusual structure adds a layer to the interior, with the glass extending beyond it. The bold shape makes a spectacular focal point visible from both inside and out.

PERFECT LIGHT

Good homes only get better when they take advantage of light. Sunlight is often employed to create an image of perfection. A minimalist, modern interior lined with beautiful materials depends on the sun to achieve its purposes. Without the distractions of decorations, the light of the sun, ever changing through the day and across the year, brings to life magnificent and animated interiors. The power of the sun has a similarly magical effect on simple modern exteriors composed of strong volumes and clear profiles. Owners are known to walk outside at dawn or at sunset to observe the perfect light's effect on their homes, just as other people would head out to view the ocean.

Windows in a modern house can be strategically positioned, sized, and detailed to bring the right effect to bear on the exterior and interior and to manipulate the flow of sunlight into specific patterns and environments. Unlike traditional houses, modern dwellings allow almost complete flexibility in the size, type, and placement of windows. The ability to create the sense of perfect light does not depend on expensive materials or complicated construction. The progression of light across a yellow pine floor, as modulated by the pattern of the windows, can be enough to make a simple room look and feel wonderful. Rooms that are positioned and fenestrated to radiate with the dappled light of a woodland setting will be no less wonderful whether they are lined in birds-eye maple or plywood.

The evening sky, with the light of the stars and the moon, can make homes even more enchanting than they are in the daytime. Artificial lighting can make every home a jack-o-lantern. Striking compositions of windows that please or challenge the eye during the day can present a fascinating display of planes of light at night. The architecture of a romantic home is often defined by a few dramatic details that are blended into the overall composition of the house by limiting the colors and materials. With perfect lighting, these details can be highlighted at night, allowing them to stand out as theatrical sculpture.

ABOVE In a modern home, even ordinary lights on the interior serve to emphasize the composition of glass openings. They can create a jack-o'-lantern effect.

LEFT Because illumination is so important in modern design, interesting ways of providing artificial lighting are esteemed. These decorative lamps are made of white pine dowels and translucent glass.

ABOVE Artificial lighting causes a roof, already large, to appear even more prominent at night. Redwood surfaces and corrugated metal are invigorated by the light.

RIGHT Transparent, well-lit modern structures stand out against a dark sky, often becoming more impressive than they are during the day. The spaces in between can be delineated by the light.

ABOVE A pool of light bathes the living room, making a sensual oasis as dusk arrives. Transparency in modern design transforms interiors into showplaces.

LEFT A layer of light, whether natural or artificial, can make an interior space cozy, as exemplified by warm light from the side at the top of a landing.

PRECEDING PAGES A row of clerestory windows becomes extraordinary at night, when the wood seems to emit a yellow-orange glow. Effective lighting maximizes the effect of exposed structure.

PART II
ROMANTIC TECHNIQUES

Peter Bohlin's Tunipus Compound at Goosewing Farm.

The quintessential romantic house is a cottage nestled in the woods or overlooking the sea. It might have a steeply pitched roof embellished with dormers, and it may feature old-fashioned adornments such as window shutters and porch posts—perhaps even a weather vane. Most of us are drawn to a house of this sort because it appeals to something deeply rooted in our emotional makeup: it arouses feelings that we associate with a good home. Romantic homes can be sentimental; they do not shy away from allegorical details. But they are not defined by those elements either. The defining feature of the romantic house is its ability to stir people's senses.

How to create a romantic house should not be the big mystery that it currently is for most people. In this section, I lay out a series of techniques you can use to design a house that's expressive and emotionally satisfying Ideally, you would build the house in a setting that intimately relates to nature, since natural scenery—particularly a view of a valley, mountains, shoreline, or luxuriant vegetation—always stirs an emotional response. The house ought to seem at ease in its setting, which means it might lie partly concealed in earth and vegetation or might have only its roof and chimneys visible above the tree-tops as you approach. It might be positioned so that a visitor glimpses the house first from one direction, then from another; the path toward the entrance can tantalize the visitor with a succession of skillfully circumscribed and choreographed views. "The approach is like the roll of the drums," says Hugh Newell Jacobsen. In a conventional urban or suburban location, the possibilities are more constrained, yet even a small site often has the potential to incorporate a garden, an area left to grow wild, water, rocks, or some other feature that will summon up associations with nature and help create an enticing and not entirely predictable entry sequence. Wherever it's placed, the house should be imbued with sentiment.

Irregularity and surprise are important parts of the picturesque approach to design. The irregularity may take the form of unusual proportions—an exceptionally tall roof, or thinner-than-normal windows, or porch posts larger than structural necessity would dictate. The surprise may also come when a cozy entrance leads to a soaring interior, which in turn contains a diminutive alcove or an unusual staircase. There should be things that spark curiosity. Most houses oversell the big door and the grand façade—features that are not essential for stirring a response.

If a pair of shutters flanking a window will make the homeowners or their guests feel joyful or contented, the designer may well add them, regardless of whether they're necessary to protect against the weather. Materials, both inside and out, should be seductive; they should have a sensual quality, causing people to want to touch them or gaze at them. Natural materials such as wood and stone are especially effective at achieving this effect.

You can bring portions of nature indoors, either literally or figuratively. A house with a log wall is one example; the logs link the home to trees outdoors; at the same time, they give the house a hardy, rough-hewn personality. One advantage of materials from nature is that they open up the potential for many varieties of expression. Natural materials left rough and primitive generate one sensation; natural materials that have been smoothed and refined create quite another. Stonework might consist of chunky, odd-shaped boulders if a rustic atmosphere is the objective. They might be rocks that fit precisely together if you want a sense of order and sophistication. The feeling differs, but in each case, the inhabitants of the home will revel in a connection to nature.

Just as the approach to the house should be carefully orchestrated, movement through the interior should be manipulated to stir emotions or establish a mood. In many houses today, you open the front door and all the living areas are exposed to your gaze. Poof, the effect is finished. It's much better if you orchestrate a sequence of experiences. In a house by Obie Bowman, you may find yourself enveloped in a forest of gigantic log columns, then led into a cave-like space, and then—bang!—comes a stunning view, maybe a view of the ocean, perhaps just a graceful old oak tree. A good home doesn't have just one kind of space; it has a variety of them, organized so that movement from one to another is full of interest and incident.

Jacobsen, Bowman, and Peter Bohlin, the architects of the homes featured here, have collaborated with their clients to create unique designs that are both modern and romantic. Their homes have few, if any, traditional details, yet they convey as much sentiment as houses composed of more old-fashioned elements. The power of these homes to bring forth a broad range of emotions—from delight to curiosity to tranquility—comes from romantic techniques such as a carefully planned approach, thoughtful manipulation of how you move through the interior, and a reward at the end of the journey.

The romantic modernist will often tap into the seductive quality of natural materials such as wood and stone and may also find expressive character in raw construction materials such as metal and untreated concrete. Unlike the picturesque movement of the nineteenth century, which used decorative details and motifs to represent nature, the modernist uses the real thing, either by capturing expansive views of the natural surroundings or by incorporating boulders, tree trunks, and other specimens of nature into the house's construction. Bohlin's own home in northern Pennsylvania rests on a large stone. "It would have been so easy to move the house or cut the stone," Bohlin says. "But the house is so much better, so much more interesting, by accommodating the stone."

Romantic techniques can make people sigh with delight or cry with surprise. They go a long way toward creating the good home.

BLENDING
INTO THE LANDSCAPE

One of the finest compliments a new house can be given is that it appears to have always been there—that it looks "natural" in its setting. Looking as if it belongs is universally understood as a good thing. Yet most houses do not give that impression at all. Conventional building practices more often go in the opposite direction. Many builders go to great lengths to keep natural elements away from houses; they tame unruly landscapes, they raise the floors high off the damp ground, and they do their best to block the effects of hot sun, cold air, snow, and rain.

Romantic designers, by contrast, want to provide all the comforts of shelter while bringing the homeowners as close to nature as possible. Some romantic homes take the notion of being in touch with the landscape literally. Obie Bowman has designed grass-covered roofs, or tucked the house into the side of a cliff, or squeezed the house in between stands of trees. The aim of many romantic designers is to achieve a seamless connection between house and ground. In this approach, mature existing plantings are preserved wherever possible; they become focal points visible from the interior and, in some instances, elements around which the exterior is composed. A romantic architect may engineer the house to allow stones or trees to remain in their original locations, with the house built around them.

Another way of fitting into the landscape involves choosing colors and materials that blend the house into its setting. The design may not be subservient to the shape of the land, yet coloration and texture tie the house to the site. Still another technique involves positioning and laying out the house and designing its silhouette in relation to the existing or intended landscape but letting the house read as a clearly independent object. Hugh Newell Jacobsen's all-white houses often do this. When seen from the landscape, they clearly belong even though they stand out. There is no one single way to blend a home into the landscape; a variety of techniques can achieve that result.

ABOVE A house adopts the self-effacing technique of merging into the landscape, letting a covering of vegetation grow up over the roof. This low-profile tactic creates a distant view that pays respect to nature.

LEFT Peter Bohlin believes in "accommodation," leaving the rock in place and building directly on it. In a poetic manner, a column that rests on the rock is splintered into several supports, highlighting the massiveness of the rock.

ABOVE The landscape here is jagged, and the house mimics its jaggedness. The house has eye-catching shapes, but does not insist upon being the main attraction. It is half tucked into the vegetation.

LEFT A house uses rustic features, including a randomly laid stone base, to harmonize with the landscape. The log column in the center of the façade echoes and pays tribute to the surrounding trees.

ABOVE A house on a cliff hunkers down below the broad-spreading canopy of a tree. The landscape, not the house, is the focus of attention.

RIGHT With foresight, a house can be planned around existing trees, as in this elegant example by Hugh Newell Jacobsen. The deck cantilevers over the roots, allowing the craggy tree to become a beautiful counterpoint to the house's crisp forms.

ABOVE An example of how a house can defer to the land. Obie Bowman has mastered the art of letting the earth extend right up onto the roof of the house.

LEFT The broad, soothing porch has a tropical quality, suggesting a man-made equivalent of the shady area beneath a tree. In this way, a house can reflect the climate of its landscape.

ABOVE A house keeps a low profile so that it does not compete with the terrain. From a distance, the house appears to nestle into its natural setting.

ABOVE   A gravel path and a wall made of concrete work well with the rocks and grasses of the abutting landscape. When the tone of the landscape is echoed in the building and paving materials, a house blends with its surroundings.

ABOVE A corridor in the landscape frames a view of a house straight on. If the landscape had a regimented allée of trees, the view would be extremely formal. This view is softer because the vegetation has been left in more or less natural condition.

LEFT A house looks perfectly relaxed in its setting, sitting low beneath the trees, framed by segments of a stone wall.

CONTROLLING THE APPROACH

A romantic architect makes a house expressive not only by designing the house according to lay of the land but also by controlling the way you move through the land to get to the house and by controlling what you see of the house as you do. Like designers of picturesque gardens, romantic architects prefer to keep the house from revealing itself in its entirety until a magic moment arrives; the buildup is almost like a striptease. A small part of the home is revealed from a distance; then a bend in the driveway may reveal a different, slightly larger part; and finally at another turn, the visitor sees the house in its entirety—dead on or at an angle, depending upon the results desired.

The seemingly pretentious movie scenes that feature an architect crouching down, wandering this way and that, and climbing a tree, trying to get the "feel of the land," are less exaggerated than you might think. A romantic architect wants to gain an intimate knowledge of the contours and qualities of the site and to control the approach. Ultimately, the approach is often laid out according to one of two models. The formal model calls for the entire house to be seen head on; in this method, the entrance is obvious. The picturesque method calls for the house to be seen from an angle or to be partly obscured. The entrance has to be searched for or is revealed subtly.

The picturesque approach is cinematic, and it enhances the qualities of the home and the property as a whole. It calls for imagining all the different experiences that a person could have on the way in. This might include giving the visitor a view of a garden gate with no house in sight, followed by a path that seems to lead to just a corner of the house, and then a spot where a big tree blocks the path, forcing a turn that reveals the front porch. Such experiences can be orchestrated on surprisingly small parcels of land leading to the most modest of homes.

ABOVE *The approach leads toward and then curves past a modest part of what is actually a sizable house. Passing through the opening in the stone wall makes approaching the home an event. Later comes a view of the water.*

LEFT *A movie-like sequence shows how an elaborate house at first seems an almost incidental part of the landscape, then becomes a strong object when viewed head on, and becomes still more impressive when experienced from the smooth court.*

ABOVE This perspective emphasizes the primacy of the natural landscape and the house's position as a kind of refuge within it.

LEFT The angled approach from a distance creates an air of mystery. Where is the front door? With relief, the visitor discovers the wooden footbridge, which leads directly to the entrance.

LEFT Once the visitor to the
Peter Bohlin house shown on Page
84 comes inside, he finds the
interior continuing the corridor-like
effect that began on the footbridge.
The entry path offers a controlled
but welcoming environment,
emotionally warm because of the
wood glowing in the sun.

RIGHT The approach to a
Hugh Newell Jacobsen house
reveals a series of pavilions, each of
equal prominence, sitting in a
serene landscape of tall trees.

BOTTOM RIGHT As the
visitor comes closer, the path leads
into a slot between two pavilions.
The narrow slot envelops the visitor
and provides a sense of arrival in a
reclusive but dignified little space.

MANIPULATING
CIRCULATION

The feeling you get from a house is heavily influenced by how you move through its interior. In a romantic home, the aim is to foster patterns of circulation that will help make the house emotionally engaging. The layout of rooms, passages, and openings should force people to move through the house in a particular way.

Hugh Newell Jacobsen sometimes divides a house into a series of buildings, each containing one or two rooms, and connects them with a series of glass breezeways, just to make sure that it's as exciting to move through the house as to settle down within it. Peter Bohlin creates a home consisting mainly of one big room with an open floor plan; within it he then creates an area that from certain angles looks like a long corridor extending from one end of the house to the other. This forces movement to follow a carefully orchestrated path that draws attention to views of the landscape and emphasize special spots on the interior.

People are often attracted to sunken living rooms. What makes a sunken living room appealing is that you need to climb down into them. Although changes of levels throughout a design may not be practical for every homeowner, where they appear, they add delight. Obie Bowman designed a California house in which the visitor is immediately forced to turn the corner, climb a few steps, and turn again before discovering the living room. The twists and turns not only make the house fun to explore; they make the living room, with its breathtaking view of the Pacific, seem even more special upon arrival.

Staircases can be designed to give interesting overlooks, at times splashed with sunlight. Landings should be seen as opportunities, because with a bit of enlargement or embellishment or outlooks, they become distinctive places within a home. When paths intersect at a landing, the designer can make it a pivot point possessing great character. Moving through the house should be an experience, one that offers a variety of sensations. Architecture comes to life through movement that attracts your interest and engages your feelings.

LEFT An open staircase offering views in all directions makes every movement through this house stimulating. The play of sunlight on circulation spaces and adjoining areas enhances the experience.

ABOVE An angle toward the end of a passage, with a space around the corner, makes movement more interesting than a walk down a straight corridor.

LEFT *Going up and down
stairs and continuing around a
corner can make a part of the house
feel special. As this interior shows,
the circulation does not have to be
arranged in the most direct path
possible. A more involved route may
add to the pleasure. Openings off
the circulation route modulate the
views and make progression through
the interior more enjoyable.*

ABOVE Having to find your way around the big column at the base of the stairs makes every trip through the interior more of an event. The column gives people an interesting object to touch or rest against, engaging another sense. The open railing lets anyone at the right watch people move through—another source of visual interest.

LEFT A corridor gains interest by passing inviting spaces on one side and then another. The protruding logs become a marker on journeys through the house. Glass at the end of the passage provides light and a view, pulling the person forward. The designer needs to consider whether the glassy end-wall will produce undesirable glare.

ABOVE A small landing makes an interesting intersection where people turn, continue straight on, or occasionally rest. In this house, people experience various spaces as they go, and enjoy a view of the outdoors.

LEFT The spiraling motion of the stairs adds another dimension to movement. At the same time, it directs a person's gaze outdoors. The climb inside the house is coordinated with the hill outside.

WORSHIPING NATURE FROM WITHIN

It might seem a stretch to say that a house or its occupants "worship" nature. But the romantic temperament takes enormous delight in earth, sky, sunlight, water, trees, flowers, and plant life of all kinds. A good home ought to express heartfelt feelings about nature, not only through the way the house looks on the outside, where it meets the land, but through the character of its interior as well.

One of the ways this is accomplished is by offering eye-catching connections between the interior living spaces and whatever lies beyond. A romantic responds to the idea of floor-to-ceiling glass or a sitting area extending outward toward the trees or an assemblage of corner windows that dissolves any sense of confinement. While sitting inside, you can be visually immersed in a rainstorm, snowfall, or bright, sunny weather. The goal, in at least part of the home, is to blur the distinction between indoors and out. The connection to nature intensifies when materials on the inside, such as a stone floor, continue beyond the house's walls. At the same time, it's a good idea to have some spaces that feel sheltered from the outdoors. Contrasts of feeling—openness and exposure in some areas, coziness and retreat in others—help make a home romantic.

Natural materials may be employed on the interior. Wood and stone communicate a sense of reverence toward nature. So does any natural material that's used as part of the house's structure, such as wood posts, beams, and brackets. Really mesmerizing emotional effects come, however, when nature in all its roughness is brought inside—as a wall built of logs, as a rock face, or some other element not wholly smoothed, tamed, and made mild.

In some instances, the structure may evoke the character of nature. Beams and brackets that support a roof may echo the lines of tree limbs. A column may suggest a tree trunk. Analogies such as these can enrich a home's emotional repertoire. Where possible, existing natural features, such as a stone outcropping, might be retained and incorporated into the house. In a romantic home, nature is close by.

ABOVE The bathtub is placed next to a sheltered window that lets the bather relax with a colorful view of flowers and plants.

LEFT A tree trunk that was found on the property makes a magnificent feature in a house by Obie Bowman.

ABOVE The use of materials from nature ties this house to its woodland setting. Details from the interior continue outside so that the house feels like an integral part of its environment. Note the roof brackets, which echo the shapes of the porch roof.

ABOVE   The angled wall of glass pushes the interior out, blurring the demarcation between indoors and outdoors. The house seeks to become part of nature.

LEFT The floor flows ever so smoothly from the living room out to the patio and landscape, giving the view of nature primacy. A generous corner of glass is an effective tool for breaking up a house's solidity and making nature the center of attention.

TOP RIGHT Chunks of driftwood logs bring nature indoors. Complementing this, a round window funnels a view through a cliff and toward the water below.

BOTTOM RIGHT A large stone detail frames a fireplace. The stone, which is part of a shower, makes showering feel like an activity in the great outdoors.

LEFT The walls are so clear and translucent that the house melds with nature. Living here has a dramatic quality, a sense of hanging over the landscape.

TOP RIGHT A greenhouse-type roof makes the treetops feel like part of the interior.

BOTTOM RIGHT A view through a thin-mullioned window to a pond. The interior requires fewer decorative effects when the focal point is the landscape.

SEDUCTIVE MATERIALS

In the nineteenth century, when the world was in the midst of the industrial revolution, romantic designers countered the machine age by designing homes and furniture that highlighted beautiful materials such as handcrafted wood, handmade ceramic tiles, and blown glass. Those old-fashioned arts and crafts not only incorporated motifs relating to nature; they employed rich natural materials in their construction. Modern romantics are similarly fascinated by seductive natural materials such as wood and stone. However, today's architects don't stop there; they also admire the picturesque qualities of materials such as concrete, metal, and masonry.

Natural materials appear at their best when put together in the most practical way given their makeup. Granite stones can be nicely chiseled into blocks, so they look best when assembled like an old stone wall. Traditional methods are not the only way, however. A good modern architect may use materials in a more innovative fashion, to tell a story or make an impression. The architect knows that wood for siding can be cut and carved in a hundred ways that will show off its rich texture and soft profiles while still standing up to the elements. A modern romantic may take common building components such as bricks and stack them to form elegant patterns— without the custom shapes or details that a nineteenth-century romantic would have used. Concrete can be poured into rough

wood forms with a raised grain to produce wonderful, soft-looking wood patterns.

Two or three contrasting materials can become even more seductive when combined in a simple composition. Set against a glossy all-white interior, a slate floor appears richer than the most extravagant marble. A touch of elegant stainless steel or nickel on its details will make a staircase of inexpensive concrete seem exotic. A material that may not seem in keeping with a home's other materials may be introduced as a way of creating a focal point. A fireplace assembled from industrial materials will have a bigger impact than one made of stone when added to a cottage in which stone and wood abound. What matters is that the materials exude feeling.

ABOVE Stones possess sensual appeal because of their color, their irregular shapes, and the patterns they form both with one another and with sunlight or artificial light. Big rough-hewn blocks over window openings make a wall look as if it's stood there for many years.

LEFT An industrial material—Corten steel—has what architects would call "a dialogue" with the cedar of the seat. The two materials together emphasize the character of each other. Many materials can be allowed to show their age.

ABOVE Concrete takes its character from the forms, usually made of wood, that surround it when it's poured. The texture and pattern of the wood forms can be chosen to generate many different effects. The thin-profile roof sits on industrial metal brackets.

LEFT This is what's called "novelty" siding. The pattern, chosen for its beauty, produces soft profiles that are very appealing. Here the siding is painted white, against which the contrasting green window trim pops out.

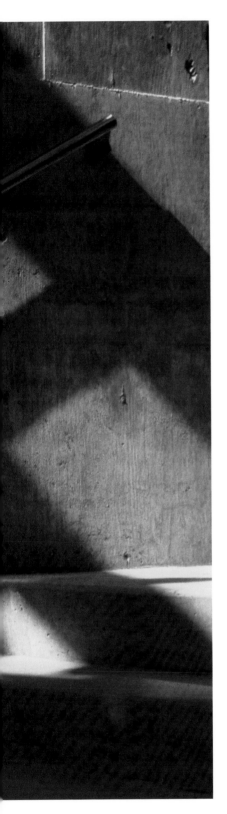

ABOVE The ends of a few charcoal-colored clinker bricks protrude from a wall of smooth red bricks. The tones of the two kinds of brick contrast nicely, and the two- and three-dimensional patterns give the wall visual punch.

LEFT The roughness of poured concrete against the smoothness of a polished-steel handrail makes a striking combination. Both materials become more seductive through juxtaposition.

ABOVE Redwood on a deck, on board and batten siding, and on a sliding barn door gives a natural and warm quality to a courtyard. With such appealing materials on so many conspicuous surfaces, asphalt composition shingles suffice on the roof.

ABOVE The concrete in this home exudes a natural feeling because it's been poured to take the pattern of wood forms. The interior stirs an emotional response because of its concrete and wood.

PART III
EVOKING THE FAMILIAR

Obie Bowman's sketch of Pin Sur Mer.

All the houses collected in this book are modern. They are filled with natural light and views, thanks to large expanses of glass. They are built in a modern mode that favors simplicity and minimalism, even if they make extensive use of traditional residential materials such as wood, brick, and stone. All of this, in my opinion, is good. So the question is, how do modern houses become modern romantic homes—dwellings that will tap into people's feelings and engage their emotions? One of the most effective methods I've found involves having the new house evoke buildings and places that people are familiar with. If a new house brings to mind buildings or places that people already know and are fond of, the owners—and visitors, too—will feel attachment.

Peter Bohlin, Hugh Newell Jacobsen, and Obie Bowman, as modern architects, do not copy buildings from the past. They create houses that are unique, in most instances strikingly so. Yet the houses these three produce connect with people's sentiments, in large part because the designs summon up associations with historical or vernacular houses; they suggest something of the character of traditional houses or rural buildings, usually in the same region where the new houses are being built.

The shape of the house is the most basic tool for evoking the familiar. Countless "no-frills" center-hall colonials and saltboxes come into being every year because their shapes suggest classic all-American homes, satisfying people's understandings of what a house should be. In many cases, it's worth noting that although profiles of historical house styles are discernible in the new tract houses, the detailing that accompanied those shapes two or three centuries ago is absent, so although the new construction reads as a traditional home, it seems anemic—a weak and bland copy of the original.

Modern romantics approach the design process in a different way. They aren't interested in simply imitating houses from the past. They may use familiar silhouettes from older buildings, and may even group several such silhouettes together, but they give the houses fresh touches too, because they don't want the results to be boring. Modern romantics want to create something new and imaginative, no matter how much of the familiar may also be perceptible in the composition. Houses by Bohlin, Jacobsen, and Bowman recall shapes that people are accustomed to, but, equally important, they exhibit the passion, ingenuity, or humor that separates distinctive homes from cookie-cutter designs.

Each traditional shape possesses its own character. A skillful designer recognizes that character and works with it. Colonials and saltboxes have strong, simple profiles that are well suited to conveying a prim and proper expression; they may suggest a historic place or an established family. A cabin in the woods or a ranch-style house is a more relaxed source of imagery; it befits a more casual or rustic expression. Historically, houses often mimicked the shapes of religious buildings, as when the physical attributes of Gothic churches and Greek temples were applied to residences, for a theatrical kind of expression. The architects featured here often borrow and reinterpret the shapes of American agricultural buildings such as barns, grain silos, storage sheds, and lean-tos. You might question whether such shapes are appropriate for the homes of human beings, but I find them stimulating and usually successful. The advantage of such shapes is that they are familiar and yet they widen the variety of expression; they make possible a composition that's completely modern without being too disconcerting. Shapes can be derived from all sorts of sources.

Modern houses run the risk of feeling alien or weird if they utterly disregard convention. Consequently, in addition to playing with familiar shapes, the romantic modern house often uses elements such as columns, chimneys, windows, and siding patterns in ways that are familiar yet imaginative. The columns or chimneys may be greatly simplified, or they may have a rustic character, depending on the feeling the house is meant to express. Decorators use salvaged pieces of old houses, such as Victorian posts or brackets, as ornamental elements and artistic focal points in contemporary interiors. If the entire interior were Victorian in style, these elements would lose their impact. Employed strategically, however, they have a strong positive effect. For some of his rustic houses, Bowman has used sliding barn doors and timber columns that look like they were retrieved from construction sites. Jacobsen's refined designs in the eastern U.S. and Canada repeat one traditional compositional element over and over again on his stark white buildings as if it were a wallpaper pattern. Bohlin blends traditional elements such as old-fashioned window and door trim with extraordinarily modern windows and doors in his woodland homes. These contrasts help generate a romantic feeling.

The romantic house challenges you; it makes you stop and wonder. In this kind of house, the pure forms and abstract patterns of modernism are layered with picturesque touches. Often there is something intentionally odd about how the familiar or sentimental elements are used in the design. The chimney may be way too large for the house. The columns may be too few or too many to be holding up the porch roof. The windows may be off center. These peculiarities are there to hold your attention, to interest you each time you look at the house. They may also be there to express the uniqueness of the homeowner, the designer, or the site.

A pair of giant columns on a small house may express a certain haughtiness, while a series of curiously small windows on a large house may express humility. Symmetrical arrangements of odd renditions of familiar elements can make them less off-putting, yet still challenging. The same is true of seemingly haphazard arrangements of traditional elements. The goal of the modern romantic is to infuse character and delight into a home without abandoning the elegance, simplicity, and up-to-date spirit of modern design. Evoking and playing with the familiar make this combination possible.

GAFFNEY RESIDENCE

What the eye first gravitates toward in the Gaffney house is its tallest and most traditional element: a three-story façade of red cedar with semi-transparent stain that sits beneath a steep roof. The gable roof and the set of four-pane windows underneath it give this house in Romansville, Pennsylvania, a comforting sense of the familiar. But familiar in what way? Devoid of ornament, almost shorn of overhangs, does the Gaffney home recall a farmhouse, or does it bring to mind a barn? This house seems familiar, yet at the same time enigmatic.

Soon your eye moves toward a strikingly modern and transparent corner that dissolves the division between indoors and out. After taking in that two-story expanse of horizontally proportioned glass, you notice that the house

doesn't stop there. To the right appears an irregular extension consisting not so much of solid walls as of big, revealing sheets of glass. These last forms have a free, organic feeling, more irregular than the three-story portion that first caught your eye.

Only after you've taken in all of this do you notice that far to the left is another appendage—a glass-topped area that butts up against a stone wall. Peter Bohlin's Gaffney residence is a remarkable compound of contrasting building forms and varied window shapes. Gables are not symmetrical. Windows do not quite line up. The plan is lightly skewed to accommodate views into the Chester County landscape. Bohlin believes that such subtle juxtapositions and distortions create a dreamlike ambience, stimulating the client's memories of experiences abroad and of childhood on a Midwestern farm.

LEFT The impression of the Gaffney house changes markedly from day to night. When the sun is up, the solid, cedar-clad walls stand out most. At night, illumination in the interior turns the house into a glowing, transparent object.

ABOVE The owner and the house, which from a distance first appears almost gaunt, like some simple rural structures.

ABOVE The sloped, gabled ceiling in the master bedroom exudes a spacious, modern feeling. The cross-ties give the space some pattern and scale and make it feel a bit more secure.

RIGHT Each window is proportioned differently, pragmatically maximizing the views of the landscape. Stone walls create bounded outdoor spaces and create landscape impressions that evoke experiences the client had abroad. There's just enough visible wall above the windows to generate a partial sense of enclosure. Near the small-pane windows, a lower ceiling makes the space feel cozier.

ABOVE *A one-story stone wall and the presence of only a few, small windows in the taller, unadorned wall of wood make the western exposure reminiscent of a barn. But it is a barn with a modern glass roof overhanging the fieldstone wall.*

ABOVE The living and dining spaces are bounded by a stone wall that's appealing to look at and to touch; it's a remnant of a barn that stood here. After entering the living-dining area, a visitor finds a view to the countryside opening up through a glass corner at the opposite end of the house.

KAHN RESIDENCE

The Kahn house in Lima, Ohio at first glance harks back to nineteenth-century Gothic Revival. The board-and-batten siding and the pointed central gable seem as quaintly all-American as Grant Wood's famous "American Gothic" painting. The symmetrical chimneys, the curious oval windows, and the high porch with pairs of skinny posts evoke the past.

Yet this is no literal reproduction. Despite latticework, divided-light windows, and other elements associated with a distant time, this is a modern house—abstracted, pared down, and painted pure white rather than the earth colors that A.J. Downing advocated 150 years ago. The continual back-and-forth between strikingly modern and old-and-familiar is what makes Hugh Newell Jacobsen's design so intriguing.

The view toward the entrance makes the house look as if it's not terribly large. But when the long and elaborate side of the house comes into view, a different character emerges. Suddenly the house looms larger, becoming more of a mansion than a Gothic cottage. With its two-story bays, still more chimneys, and its powerful symmetry, the Kahn house recalls the grand houses of the past—though the impression is given an unusual modern twist by the squaring off of all the chimneys and by the placement of a skylight at the roof's peak.

The contrast between modern touches and an older character pervades the interior as well. Transparency and openness dominate some views, but other perspectives feel more traditional. This is a house of contradictions, provoking varied sensations—in one moment closed in, and in the next instant wide open and filled with light.

LEFT The narrow end of the Kahn house makes a friendly and generally old-fashioned impression, but the squared-off chimneys give the home a contemporary flair.

ABOVE The undulating side is much grander. The narrow, elongated windows recall those from Victorian times. The whiteness and the simplicity of the chimney shapes, however, mark this as a contemporary home.

ABOVE   The long, divided-light windows and folding wooden shutters evoke the feeling of a house from more than a century ago.

ABOVE When the shutters are folded together, the interior becomes airy, open, and bright, strongly modern in its atmosphere.

FOLLOWING PAGES At night the house becomes transparent and seems strikingly modern despite the procession of bays and divided-light windows.

WINDHOVER

indhover, at Sea Ranch in northern California, calls to mind the temple form that goes all the way back to ancient Greece. Versions of this house's great pediment, raised upon two massive columns, have appeared in thousands of banks, courthouses, churches, and (most relevant for residential design) grand houses—those that have graced American estates, plantations, and boulevards for well over 200 years.

What's most curious about Obie Bowman's design is that the strongly classical overtones are contradicted by the spareness, indeed primitiveness, of the materials and surfaces. Though the pediment above the entrance has a shape handed down through centuries of human culture, the house has a rustic air. The "columns" are tree trunks with only the bark removed. You can even tell where the branches used to grow. They give the house a muscular feeling, which is intensified by the columns' lack of either capitals or bases. The tone of the steps ties the building to the earth.

The bold temple shape helps a modest-size (1,570-square-foot) dwelling hold its own in a neighborhood of larger homes. Once you look past the columns, it becomes evident that this is, nonetheless, a thoroughly contemporary house. Glass abounds. Double-height glass beneath the pediment consists of inexpensive, stacked sliding glass doors. The interior is open and full of angles, with white gypsumboard walls contrasting against extensive areas of wood, so that although there is a hearty connection with nature, the overall esthetic is bracingly modern.

LEFT A very simple pediment of clear redwood bevel siding rests on two massive tree trunk–columns, with no capitals or bases to add decorum. The steps serve as pedestals for the columns, but their brown tone ties the house to the earth.

ABOVE The loft-like interior has a brawny feeling, with large exposed timbers running both orthogonally and at unusual angles. The overall effect is dynamic and contemporary.

LEFT The bedroom loft, with its asymmetrical skylight, features layer upon layer of wood components, which weave a pattern and generate a sense of depth. The effect resembles the intertwining of the branches in a forest.

ABOVE The fireplace is made of concrete formed from pieces of the bevel siding. The corrugated pipe makes the composition more dramatic, and it contrasts against the wall's 2-by-10 wood framing structure of Douglas fir, dyed red.

FOLLOWING PAGES Logs that drifted up from the water have been placed on bases of industrial metal, making an evocative, cave-like entrance. The lighting accentuates the entrance's depth. The modern cutaway created by expanses of glass treats the bedroom like a display case.

OLD MISSION COTTAGE

What could be more enticing than a cottage in the woods? This modest house on the western shore of Old Mission Peninsula in Lake Michigan's Grand Traverse Bay reinterprets the aged cabins the owners were fond of visiting during summer holidays. It reflects a simple and relaxed life of long, warm summer days, of quiet, cool evenings with a fire, and of sailing, reading, and baking fruit pies. The quintessential cottage shape, with a simple, steeply pitched roof sheltering the living space below, brings forth feelings that almost everyone has for cottages sitting amid the trees, their protruding roofs offering protection from the elements.

By enlarging the roof beyond usual cottage dimensions, Peter Bohlin magnifies the cottage image and at the same time makes way for a much more expansive interior. The series of doors on the front evokes something familiar—perhaps a camp dining hall where people gather for meals and conversation. The posts and beams are rugged, yet artful. The flaring, exaggerated brackets attached to the posts seem fanciful and light-hearted—a fitting emotion for a getaway place.

Approach closer and what next commands attention is the capacious steps—broader than the house itself. They extend outward in three directions in a welcoming gesture. Some might see them as a kind of waterfall in wood. At the same time, they bring to mind gregarious spots like amphitheaters and the steps of college buildings, where people relax while looking outward. The components of this house seem familiar, yet the ensemble is fresh and pleasurably surprising.

LEFT The big gable roof evokes a sense of shelter and domesticity. Gables can be used in imaginative ways and in radically differing sizes.

ABOVE The cottage reaches out with cascading wooden steps. Their tone distinguishes them from the ground. They seem to elevate the house, making it grander, while also harmonizing with the galvanized metal roof.

LEFT *The exposed rafters bring to mind rustic camp buildings and the welcome sense of shelter they provide. The walls accentuate the feeling that this is a cabin in the woods.*

ABOVE *Repetitive patterning, including the suggestion of grid upon grid through the far window, takes this house beyond the realm of elementary shelter. Note the gnarled tree trunk at the entrance to the room; here architecture worships nature..*

LEFT Dimness can produces a sense of refuge, while translucent wall panels create a bright area in an otherwise wooden, cabin-like interior. A pitched ceiling with exposed rafters seems a perfect counterpoint to the imaginatively designed concrete fireplace.

ABOVE Unlike the steps of many houses, which require people to enter and leave by a narrow, set route, these steps are generous in the freedom they offer. These steps also adapt to the undulations of the land.

PART IV
CREATING A SENSE OF PLACE

Peter Bohlin's sketch of Point House.

Romantic architects like to refer to the effects they create as "senses." A "sense of breeze" might be the experience of sitting in a room that makes you feel as if you're on a breezy tropical island, when in fact you're in a northern city. A "sense of height" is the feeling that a room or space or building is very tall, far beyond its actual dimensions. One of the perceptions that designers especially prize is a "sense of place"—the feeling that you're somewhere special, whether it's on top of a mountain or in a town square. A romantic house can create a sense of place even if the property is not large, does not possess a panoramic view, and does not comprise an entire compound.

The predominant way of creating a "sense" is by intensifying people's perceptions. You can create a sense of height by positioning short objects next to the walls that you want to appear tall. You can create a sense of distance by placing certain features, such as a pond, in the landscape's middle ground, thus making the background stretch farther away. To generate a sense of place, you can select the most auspicious of the locations available and then intensify the experience of getting to, and moving through, the house and the property.

A landscape architect might intensify the approach to the house by creating an *allée*—a walk or path between two rows of formally-planted trees or shrubs that are at least twice as high as the walk or path is wide. An architect tends to intensify the approach by carefully choosing where to position the house on the land and by giving the house a shape and a layout that will make it feel like a special spot. Usually there are just one or two best routes for reaching a property, whether by foot or by vehicle. Down a street or road, over a hill, or around a bend, the house comes into view. The romantic architect shapes the house and composes its windows and doors with a keen awareness of which part of the house will be seen first, second, and so on. The house may be designed to give one impression from far off and a different impression up close. For example, from a distance, visitors may not be able to discern where the front door is, but once they come near, they discover a conspicuous and welcoming entryway. This technique makes a person feel confused or curious while searching for the door, thus intensifying the delight of finding the inviting entrance once it becomes visible.

If this sounds a bit manipulative, keep in mind that romantic houses are intended to be sensual, making impressions on the occupants and visitors. A walk through a romantic house can be a journey that includes vistas, surprises, and illusions, such as short distances that seem much longer than they are, and tall spaces that seem even taller. Photography, even video photography, can rarely capture the full effect of moving in and about a romantic house, for it is an emotional experience, forged by visual, tactile, and kinetic sensations as you advance.

Once you have entered the house, the romantic architect continues massaging and managing your feelings. In Hugh Newell Jacobsen's design for the Palmedo residence, the front door is in a part of the house that stands forward from the house's main body, connected only by a glass-walled, short corridor. Its separation from the rest of the dwelling requires the guest to enter, then go through a transparent passage—in effect, to go outside again—and then walk forward to get into the main component of the house, which of course is the real destination. It's a shocking experience that intensifies the experience of arriving. The jolt is not unlike the frustrations that often accompany travel to special places. Since the journey through the front door is only for visitors (the occupants usually enter from another direction) there is no reason the entry sequence can't be a little contorted to convey a "sense of place." Obie Bowman is fond of making both the visitors and the owners climb up or down or find their way around corners after they enter a house, for no other reason than to intensify their experiences. At Peter Bohlin's own home in northeastern Pennsylvania, the sense of place is accentuated by striking views or unusual ways of presenting them, such as a kitchen window with Alice-in-Wonderland proportions, magically suspended in air.

These three modern romantics share an admiration for a modern flow of spaces, one room open to next, but arranged in just the right way so as to control your every step. The genteel homes of Jacobsen, the beatnik homes of Bowman, and the traditional-to-progressive homes of Bohlin are all built from plans that set rooms apart at angles, or that separate them with small rooms or spaces. Views or focal points pull you one way or another so that moving through a house conjures up the feeling of walking through the woods or ascending a mountain.

Jacobsen designs into each house a stunning experience that is akin to suddenly commanding a panoramic view from a mountaintop. His goal is for the visitor and the homeowner to be bowled over upon discovering it. Not everyone can do that. But a modern romantic strives to lay out a house so that a person moves through it according to a plan that leads them to a spot offering an impressive view of the countryside, a breathtaking fireplace, or just a beautiful tree. That special spot, sometimes referred to as the point of arrival, is an essential ingredient in a "sense of place."

TUNIPUS COMPOUND

A good home can use any of a number of techniques to create a sense of place. At Tunipus Compound in Little Compton, Rhode Island, the landscape—70 acres, much of it meadow, surrounded by water on three sides—sets the scene. Parts of the landscape are defined by elements such as a low concrete wall, which forms a semi-enclosed courtyard linking the guesthouse (a renovated and expanded nineteenth-century cottage) to the garage. Often people realize that a place is special when they are obliged to take a journey through its constituent parts. Here visitors must walk through an open courtyard to reach the house's entrance. Even a journey of a few dozen feet registers on people's consciousness.

Peter Bohlin designed Tunipus Compound with broad, uninterrupted slopes of roof that allow the upper portions of the walls to retreat into shadow. Mild colors, undemanding shapes, familiar materials such as cedar shingles, and a semi-protected courtyard all contribute to the sense that this home is a refuge.

What causes Tunipus Compound to rise above the ordinary is the surprises that unfold upon venturing into the house. The interior, though sheltering, is unmistakably modern. The ceiling was peeled away to reveal the joists. The wall practically evaporates around a prominent fireplace framed by views into the landscape beyond. Once a warren of small rooms, the interior now is open and spacious. The crispness of the interior leaves no doubt that this is, after all, a distinctive setting.

LEFT The simple slope of a cedar shake roof and the quiet exterior walls, seen across a meadow, make Tunipus Compound a relaxing place.

ABOVE A low concrete wall encloses a courtyard, which establishes a connection between the guesthouse in the distance and the garage in the foreground. A boardwalk from the garage to the house's front door makes approaching the entrance an event.

LEFT A glossy floor of Douglas fir and a ceiling dramatically opened up to expose recycled Douglas fir stock trusses with finish boards on the bottom chord make the interior distinctive. The ceiling opening starts narrow near the private bedroom area and widens as it approaches a fireplace in the most public part of the house.

ABOVE The progression through the house leads toward a dramatically designed fireplace, which commands attention, yet also allows people to see past it to the sunlight and trees. The slatted Douglas fir screen around the fireplace is a recurrent motif, an example of the appeal of patterns.

LEFT   A blocky chimney of zinc-coated copper, butted up against the symmetrical windows, contrasts strikingly with traditional shingles. The finish material at the lower portion of the exterior wall is cedar clapboard with a painted finish.

ABOVE   Water is a restful feature, one that usually makes a property feel larger. Because the concrete wall is weathered and eroded, the setting feels relaxed rather than pristine and formal.

PREVIOUS PAGES   The ceiling offers a mesmerizing pattern of beams and diagonal bracing. An ordinary, box-like interior has become dynamic. In every direction a person looks, the views are interesting enough to generate a sense of place.

SOHN RESIDENCE

One way to create a sense of place is to break a large house into a series of smaller components. Architects often liken the resulting components to a "village," since the overall effect resembles a cluster of individual dwellings. Hugh Newell Jacobsen, a master of such assemblages, used that technique in the playful Sohn residence overlooking Lake Simcoe in southern Ontario.

Whereas a conventional house has a front, a back, and two sides, the Sohn residence is variegated, containing a series of spaces between segments, making the dwelling less of a monolith and more of a "place." The $1^{1/2}$-story components have a diminutive scale, like that of cabins in a camp. Because each unit shares the same spare esthetic

and has the same pristine white on its exterior, they read as a unified group; small variations such as differing window sizes and non-uniform chimney locations force the eye to go back and forth, measuring and comparing. This engagement with the viewer is part of the fascination of a picturesque house.

The Sohn house is traditional in its use of shapes such as gabled roofs and prominent chimneys and in its choice of divided-light windows, but it is undeniably modern in its abstraction and in its severe detailing. Ornament is almost entirely absent. Chimneys are clad in tongue-and-groove clear cedar—very smooth. On the interior, the variety of spaces reinforces the sense of place even while the pervasive whiteness, the openness to the landscape, and the abundance of sunlight mark this as a truly modern design.

LEFT   The relationships among the series of components are simple, yet intriguing, drawing a person in. The entrance walkway threads into one of the passages between similar, but not identical, white gabled segments. The wood exteriors and wood chimneys unify the parts.

ABOVE   Lining up the components so that they define the edge of a shared landscape generates a village-like effect. The complex, linked by glass-walled passages, runs parallel with a treed embankment overlooking Lake Simcoe.

LEFT A spare, white interior space feels expansive because it extends all the way to the underside of the roof.

ABOVE The rhythmic window panes capture a succession of views for a picturesque effect. The lower panes frame a series of tree trunks, while upper panes capture views of their crowns. The window in the gable makes the sky yet another focal point.

ABOVE The interior becomes alluring at dusk when selective lighting makes the niches in the walls stand out. Suddenly the room achieves a feeling of depth. The design allows a simple, almost severe room to become visually rich and complex.

RIGHT The mantel evokes some of the feeling of a traditional hearth, but because it's abstracted—pared down into a simple horizontal with no moldings for support—the entire wall reads as the fireplace-surround. The modern wall-to-wall grid of bookcases bestows additional character on the room.

LEFT *The consistent whiteness belies the complexity with which some of the parts come together. The skylight-cupola above the factory-coated white aluminum roof introduces a picturesque element to the composition.*

ABOVE *The movement of sun and shadow modulates the feeling of the exterior throughout the day, and gives the simple forms interesting nuance.*

TIN ROOF

This house at Sea Ranch on the northern California coast generates a sense of place by offering the inhabitants a series of small outdoor areas sheltered from strong winds off the Pacific. The reddish concrete pavers make visitors feel that they've arrived even before they reach the entrance. The irregular path of approach—the grid of paving stones is incomplete and interspersed with vegetation—accentuates the feeling that getting to this house is something of an adventure. The guestroom door is positioned in an alcove, making a small space off a larger space—a very effective way to create a succession of experiences.

The contrast between the sheltering exterior, much of it clad in wood or in corrugated metal that conjures up associations with agricultural structures, and the interior, dramatically open and abounding in natural light, arouses a strong reaction—relief and delight—when people finally enter. The materials are familiar, but used in ways that provoke surprise, as with the corrugated metal pipe that serves as fireplace flues. A visitor's emotions oscillate between being soothed by the glowing expanses of wood and made curious by the complex ceilings and walls.

An intriguing combination of coziness and spaciousness keeps sensations alert in this interior by Obie Bowman. The biggest effects are reserved for after a person is safely ensconced indoors. Outdoors, the house doesn't try to upstage its formidable surroundings of rocky cliff, rough meadow, and weather-beaten conifers.

LEFT   The high, sheltering walls and the disarmingly irregular arrangement of plants and decorative objects, such as a salvaged cupola, make the terrace at Tin Roof a place with character. Visitors climb concrete steps (illuminated at night by a light in the dark circle in the photo's extreme right) to approach a barn-like guestroom door.

ABOVE   The house defers to the rugged, windblown landscape in this view from a distance. The integrity of the surroundings is preserved.

ABOVE Corrugated pipe and distinctive plant life make an exotic entryway.

RIGHT Reductive materials such as the wood of the floor, ceiling, and walls and the stone of the fireplace are calculated to stimulate an emotional response from the inhabitants. At the same time, the corrugated steel culvert pipes rising from the fireplace provoke curiosity; they intriguingly shroud a double flue.

LEFT Wood everywhere—on the floors, the walls, and the ceiling, not to mention the exposed beam—suffuses the bathroom with a welcoming warmth.

ABOVE The slope of the roof gives the bedroom loft an appealing snugness even though the room itself is open and receives a good deal of light.

ABOVE A house that seemed to recede into the background during the day becomes extroverted and bright at night. The framing of a vista makes the house feel in charge of its setting.

RIGHT In daytime, the house remains a quiet part of its surroundings.

TOM & KARIN'S PLACE

In a wooded setting at California's Sea Ranch, Tom & Karin's place is a small and simple main volume, but with steeply sloped appendages attached to its gray-shingled sides. These "add-ons," projecting outward and visually anchoring the building to its site, generate the sense that this is a compound of buildings. As you go around the house, the varying scale of the parts and the way they come together create unique places in an otherwise homogeneous woodland.

The way the deck with a built-in bench seat and a hot tub extends into the shaded area beneath the trees accentuates the feeling that the house is entirely at home in the landscape. The add-ons suggest familiar shapes, such as agricultural sheds. The western red cedar siding on the angular extensions further intensifies the house's sense of being at one with the surroundings.

Despite the familiar elements, Obie Bowman has created a strongly modern house, especially inside, where a cantilevered master bedroom—cliff-like and suffused with light from above—overlooks a double-height living room. Because the house has so much glass, the interior cliff is clearly visible from outside, strengthening the house's sense of belonging to the site. Grids of wood organize storage spaces on the walls. Details such as the lamp above the dining table, projecting from the bottom chord of a Douglas fir truss, introduce interesting surprises. This is a house that is loose and unpredictable, exuding almost a funhouse quality.

LEFT The appendages stop short of the roofline and the corners, thus staying visually subordinate to the house's main volume. This reduces the apparent size of the house, which has 1,595 square feet of heated space and 509 square feet of unheated space.

ABOVE Trees come close to the house, accentuating its woodsy character.

LEFT Areas of brightness lead the eye through the ground floor and up to the peak, generating curiosity and wonder. A visitor looks upward and wonders what it's like in the platform area suspended above the main floor.

ABOVE The combination of views is rich: in the foreground, the warmly gridded wall, beyond, the bedroom platform, and above, a shaft of light.

LEFT Indoors and outdoors are intimately connected. This view shows the cantilevered bedroom inside and reflections of trees on the glass.

ABOVE A spa in the woods, open to the foliage on two sides and protected by a low wooden enclosure on the other two sides.

GREENE RESIDENCE

The Greene residence on the Chesapeake Bay's eastern shore in Maryland divides a substantial house into a series of components, each with its own volume. Whereas the Sohn house in Canada is a group of gable-roofed pavilions all in a neat row, the Green house shows that pavilions can be arranged at a series of angles, thus making the collection appear even more strikingly village-like. The five pavilions gather together as if huddling against the elements; the result is a welcoming courtyard.

Pyramidal roofs give each component a conspicuous stillness, an eye-stopping stability. The walls are redolent of the restrained houses that people built in the area in the eighteenth century, their windows no larger than absolutely necessary. An atmosphere of purity and decorum pervades the setting. Hugh Newell Jacobsen turns the absence of substantial trees—ordinarily a disadvantage—into an asset, by spreading a pavement of pea gravel around the base of the structures, thereby tying everything together.

As you explore the house, the calm initial impression is contradicted by surprises such as a sheer corner of butt-jointed tinted glass giving the occupants unconstrained views of the water. The glassy cutaway corner and other details are as restrained, in modern style, as the white clapboard aesthetic is in traditional style. Upon entering, a visitor discovers that this house is anything but traditional. Soaring interiors with divided-light windows far higher than in an old house creates the drama for which the best modern romantics are famous.

LEFT   The segments of this spread-out residence meet the ground with spare, quietly contrasting forms of steps. The pea gravel all around unifies the composition.

ABOVE   The five-part house exudes restraint, perhaps even humility. The house might have overpowered the landscape if the five volumes had been a single, large structure.

ABOVE From the fireplace up, the interior soars three stories, with light from a dormer window catching the eye. Behind the free-standing fireplace wall is an open hall.

ABOVE The angled end of the fireplace wall, paneled to give it human scale and a bit of traditional feeling, leads the eye to the glassy corner of the room and out toward the bay.

ABOVE The owner's second-floor painting studio, cozy and almost colonial in scale, offers respite from the expansiveness of the main floor.

ABOVE Space flows around the main staircase in a part of the interior that exudes a loft-like feeling. The effect has a sculptural quality.

LEFT Traditional white clapboard suddenly gives way to sheet glass where the bay demands to be seen. The simplicity of traditional design meets the simplicity of the modern.

ABOVE The landscape slips past the house and at the same time tucks into the folds of the house, for inside/outside continuity. It's as if a person could step through the glass and onto the patio.

PART V
COLLABORATING WITH THE LAND

A ltering the land and the landscape is easy. Machinery can cut down a small forest or rearrange a hillside in a few days. Soft, marshy ground or solid rock that's seemingly unsuitable for building upon is a slight nuisance the homeowners can surmount if they're willing to take on some additional expense. Dry yellow deserts can be turned into lush landscapes of green almost overnight with installation of mature plantings and simple irrigation systems. So why would modern architects be at all anxious about the land and landscape when they are free of its constraints?

The answer is that the existing landscape usually possesses character—perhaps undervalued—and is more an asset than a detriment if you adopt a romantic approach to design. Romantic architects see raw, undisturbed land as a potential collaborator in the creation of unique houses, dwellings that gain much of their distinctiveness from the limitations and idiosyncrasies of the site.

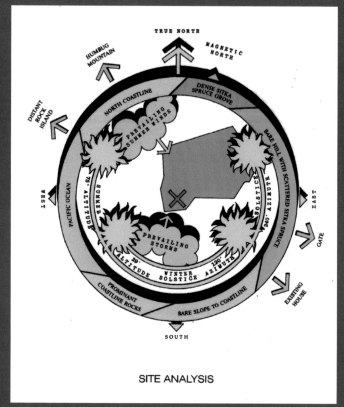

SITE ANALYSIS

Obie Bowman's study for the Oregon Coast house.

Every piece of land offers the sun, the night sky, breezes, contours, scents, sounds, colors, and the presence or absence of water. Even a property in the middle of the densest city has some relationship to nature. The ideal partner for romantic solutions is, of course, untouched countryside. A rocky cliff covered in moss or barnacles, a rolling meadow of wild grasses and flowers, a thicket of birches—these are landscapes with valuable attributes that can too easily be destroyed as the land is developed. This is why Obie Bowman frets with his "'personal paradox': a desire to build and a need to work with rather than against the natural landscape." Hugh Newell Jacobsen and Peter Bohlin operate slightly differently; they have no fear of manipulating the natural landscape, but like skilled and experienced gardeners, they begin with an intense reverence for the land's qualities.

"Worshiping nature" would not be too strong a description of the designs of these three. You can sense it in how their houses are photographed. Often the landscape, more than the architecture, seems to be the central feature. "It's the landscape that drives it," says Jacobsen, discussing the inspiration for his seemingly formal, almost rigid designs. "The secret is the garden." Bohlin's designs emerge from geometric layouts based on rules of proportion—annotated with picturesque observations about the rising and setting sun or the vistas of the landscape.

The elements—sun, wind, and weather—are fundamental aspects of nature to be respected and capitalized upon. Any home can benefit from a sunny spot for breakfast or a shady spot for spending warm summer afternoons. Interiors are designed as theaters for the play of natural light. Bowman begins every project with a personal and expressive diagram that charts each element onto a map of the property so that he can best tap into each of their potential effects. Patterns of windows become displays of sun shadows on hardwood floors. Shadowy spaces lead to intensely lit ones, like scenes in a suspense movie. Combined with other elements such as cool or fragrant breezes, the sun and shade animate the house, making one room or another a favorite spot at certain times and in certain seasons.

When skillfully harnessed, the sun exerts a powerful impact on a home's appearance. One of the most surprising features of Jacobsen's seemingly stoic houses is how expressive they become with the changing of the day. The slick surfaces of white painted wood or bricks put on new faces from morning through evening as the sun casts ever-changing shadows on the houses' sculptured exteriors, set against the surrounding landscape. In some instances, the ground itself is a focal point of romantic design. Bowman solves his paradox of building and yet preserving the landscape by wrapping his homes with the land, bringing the ground up and over the roof. Jacobsen creates great carpets of gravel to set his homes upon, recalling the good, solid surface of farmyards. For Bohlin an outcropping of rock is as glorious as any vista, and rather than frame it as a view, he pays tribute to it by "accommodating it." He does not remove it; he builds around it.

A steeply sloped site costs less to acquire than a more level one, and for the romantic architect this is a lucky break. Never satisfied with homes that permit only one expression, a romantic appreciates the ability of a steep hill to put a house low to the ground on one side and high in the air on another. This applies to interiors as well. Embracing the multiplicity of the land's traits rather than forcing uniformity onto it brings forth a more dynamic and romantic solution. Allowing vegetation, whether it's a single large tree or a marshy lowland, to be preserved or "accommodated," as Bohlin would say, is in tune with romantic ideal and also with the capabilities of modern construction. Traditional methods of building disturbed the earth, often eliminating all the plantings not only within the house's footprint but also within twenty or thirty feet of its perimeter. By using reinforced concrete, laminated wood posts and beams, steel cables, or other structural components, the modern romantic can allow large parts of their homes to float above the ground. That is one of the methods of collaborating with the land.

Whether to merge into the land, float above it, establish a man-made base, or make a strong contrast against the terrain is a choice that must be worked out for each romantic house. No matter which route is selected, in one way or another the romantic designer collaborates with the land.

OREGON COAST HOUSE

This house overlooking the Pacific Ocean at Gold Beach, Oregon, is designed with the landscape and protection from 100-mile-per-hour winds uppermost in mind. Obie Bowman organized the house so that the occupants can enjoy generous and varied views—of the ocean, of the mammoth rocks known as sea stacks that jut from the water, and of the green, often foggy coastline. The walls facing the ocean are largely transparent. But rather than being composed of sheets of glass as large as possible—the stance that modernists have often taken—most of the glazing is divided into segments that are four feet wide at most and in some instances only a couple of feet high.

The pervasive grid of wood imposes structure on the views, encouraging the eye to focus on particular parts of the scene. One window—or set of windows—frames a slice of land, another a view of sky, still another a mix of sea and sky. Besides isolating the different views, the wooden grid, with its natural tones, makes the interior feel warmer and more sheltering.

Massive log buttresses give the impression of holding the house in place, adding a dramatic sense of structural tension that makes the home feel as strong and rugged as the terrain it commands. Visually, the timbers step the house down into the landscape, grounding it. The interior contains a mix of large open spaces and intimate spots, such as a built-in window seat, where a person can nestle in and feel secure, right next to the big view.

LEFT Like the prow of a ship, the triangular end of the house looks out to sea. Window framing of various sizes, and log posts beyond, subdivide the large vista into a series of more focused views.

ABOVE Posts and diagonal buttresses of Port Orford cedar logs form a kind of exoskeleton, dramatizing the house and making it feel amply braced against the winds.

LEFT The large opening from the living room to a bedroom helps the 1,860-square-foot house feel more spacious.

ABOVE Giant timbers on the outside make the setting seem wilder by suggesting that without such structural heroics, the house might not stand.

LEFT   A structural grid wall, minimalist but warm, creates a pattern for the living room while at the same time providing useful display space.

ABOVE The bedroom can be closed off with steel-framed sliding doors. Their cement fiberboard panels have been stained with chemicals and garden-variety fertilizers for a beautiful mottled look.

ABOVE The cantilevered prow sits high enough to command views of the sea stacks and the ocean. The division of the windows into a series of panes makes the sitting area feel less vulnerable.

ABOVE Sometimes a house must be designed boldly if it's to live up to the character of its setting. Port Orford cedar log buttresses step the house at Gold Beach into the landscape.

PALMEDO RESIDENCE

Though you may not realize it instantly, given the tabletop-flat terrain, the Palmedo house on Long Island, New York, works extremely closely with its landscape. The visitor's approach is straight on, with the squared-off forecourt providing a meticulously ordered base for a perfectly symmetrical house. House and setting resonate with each other. What later bowls the visitor over is that Jacobsen has devised a sequence of movement and views that links people to the landscape at every turn.

The gabled entry portion exists principally to bring you inside and then send you through a glass-walled outdoor passage—reinforcing the primacy of the setting—before you reach the main body of the house.

Once you're fully inside, you find the walls and the generous windows arranged to bring the outdoors in. Dissolving the barriers between inside and out has long been a goal of modern architects. In the living room, a corner of butt-jointed glass running all the way down to the floor makes the walls practically melt away. The landscape—first the manmade portion, where the corner of a patio echoes the corner of the room, and then the larger natural portion, where a view of Long Island Sound is framed by trees—shows itself to be the star of the show.

By not giving away the full view at the start, by withholding parts of it, adding dynamic twists, placing some windows where they capture only sky, and then letting certain views explode outward, this home intensifies the feeling of involvement in the landscape.

LEFT The large, butt-jointed corner window allows the view to come powerfully inside the living room.

ABOVE Seen head-on from the entry drive, the house makes a strong, yet playful impression, thanks to its symmetrical but almost cartoon-like series of parts, each echoing its neighbor.

LEFT Cutting out the corner makes the view more important than the house itself. This technique makes sense in a scenic location.

ABOVE Crisp corners with virtually no overhangs make a dramatic modern volume.

ABOVE The contrast between floor-to-ceiling wall and floor-to-ceiling glass invariably draws a person to the light.

ABOVE The dining area enjoys unobstructed views through glass doors on one side and a patterned exposure to sunlight in the opposite direction.

ABOVE   The entry section stands in front of the main body of the house. The sheer glass of the connecting passage contrasts strikingly against the multitude of tiny panes in the other windows.

ABOVE At night the glow from the windows makes a beckoning impression. A staircase in the front section connects to the house's second floor.

GEORGIAN BAY RETREAT

The Georgian Bay retreat in Cedar Ridge, Ontario, fits into the trees. The aim is to intrude as little as possible on the landscape, inserting the house so that nature appears to have the upper hand. Bohlin deferred to the landscape by refraining from cutting the white birches and other trees that conceal the house in summer and that form a substantial border of trunks and branches through the winter, when the house's long, white front wall merges with the snow.

"Wall" is not quite the right word. It's really a plane, floating free, as advocated by modernists such as Mies van der Rohe. This technique reduces a wall's apparent weight and decreases the building's boxiness. Reducing the walls to planes helps to break down their bulk and let the sur-

rounding woods dominate the atmosphere all the more. Likewise, the simple slope of roof diminishes the magnitude of the roof and lets it float ever so lightly in its natural setting.

The house does arouse feelings, however. When people enter, they discover the dramatic use of exposed wood trusses, handsome details such as lines of black bolts holding the timbers together, and the beautiful effect of natural light coming in from above. The warm sheen of the wood that's employed throughout—in the post-and-beam construction, in the underside of the roof, in the flooring, and in the cabinetry—reinforces the woodland character and offers a sense of refuge from the cold. Exposed wood and articulated structure seem at home amid the trees.

LEFT The lean-to roof and the floating wall plane take the massiveness out of the house and allow nature to appear untrampled-upon.

ABOVE The long white wall blends in with the snow and the birches, making the house a comfortable part of the woodland.

FOLLOWING PAGES Exposed wood structure make the house feel well-suited to its surroundings.

ABOVE Exposed structure, which might be considered a modernist characteristic, doubles as a beautiful, intricate pattern in the central corridor.

ABOVE An alcove-like family room along the corridor feels like an extension of a log cabin.

LEFT The house seems reclusive with its wall nestled behind the vegetation and with the roof practically disappearing into shadow.

ABOVE An orange glow, like that of embers in a campfire, evokes the feeling of being outdoors.

MCKINNEY HOUSE

Another way to collaborate with the landscape is to insert the house tightly into the trees and use modernist construction techniques that avoid touching the ground. In the McKinney house on Figure Eight Island on the Outer Banks of North Carolina, Jacobsen runs a wood deck out from the perimeter of the house, letting people perch among the sunlight and vegetation and allowing the house to feel like it's delicately floating rather than subjugating the land. Decks are inherently lighter in feeling than traditional porches, which rest with a fully expressed heaviness of gravity upon the soil.

Where a mature tree stands, the deck has been built around it, amplifying the feeling that the house is subordinate to the landscape. In instances like this, the tree becomes more than just a tree; it becomes a kind of living sculpture, its form celebrated by being allowed to rise through the flooring. It provokes the realization that the house, which is usually conceived as permanent, has been rendered subservient to nature, whose individual specimens are temporary but whose realm outlasts the dwellings of human beings.

Abstraction and glass, both used to great effect by modernists over the decades, can reduce a house's imprint on its setting. In the McKinney home, gable endwalls are completely opened up, diminishing the building's mass and also making the outdoors a more powerful visual and emotional influence on the inhabitants. In a house like this, people live outdoors much of the time, and even when they retreat to the interior, they still feel connected to the great outdoors.

LEFT The cantilevering of the deck avoids damaging the root systems and lets people feel as if they're living in the trees.

ABOVE The roofscape, with its chimneys, makes a strong impression, but because the house is engulfed in foliage, the landscape loses none of its lush appeal.

ABOVE Pavilions with a bridge-like connection make minimal intrusions on the landscape. The multiple-pane window is a familiar object to be lingered over, whereas the gable containing a triangle of glass is emphatically a bold shape.

ABOVE The eye insists on going out when there are no dividers in the glass to stop it and when the deck outside seems a natural continuation of the floor.

LEFT Building the deck around mature trees ties the house to the landscape, greatly enhancing the enjoyment that people get from it.

RIGHT The walls and ceiling look so light that they might fly away in a breeze. Abstracted forms seem relatively weightless.

BELOW RIGHT A tree very close to the house casts a dappled light, softening the solid surfaces.

PINS SUR MER

rank Lloyd Wright believed the proper place to build a house was on the brow of a hill rather than on top of it. That way, the occupants would enjoy the view, but landscape would remain dominant and undefiled. In one sense, Pins Sur Mer by Obie Bowman, overlooking Schooner Gulch and Bowling Ball Beach in Point Arena, California, violates Wright's dictum; it stands on the top of a bluff above the Pacific. But Pins Sur Mer—roughly, Pines on the Sea—actually is more reticent than some of Wright's designs. Though the house occupies a fantastic setting, the dwelling hunkers down in a stand of evergreens, almost completely hidden. This is a masterly example of the art of staying in the background and letting nature remain the primary attraction.

The house form itself epitomizes calm. The gently pitched hip roof makes a soothing presence, deferring to the drama of nature's spectacle. The roof hovers above walls of glass, which maximize the occupants' enjoyment of the stunning locale.

Despite the avoidance of flamboyance on the exterior, the house is full of feeling within. Great tree trunks rise in its center. Their heft and their placement at the core of the home make it seem that the house is not just in harmony with nature; it worships nature. The tree columns are so majestic, they could be the supports of a rustic temple. The extensive use of Douglas fir amplifies the sense that the house is both of nature and in nature.

LEFT Pins Sur Mer sits inconspicuously amid a grove of Bishop pines, preserving the drama of the oceanside bluff.

ABOVE The house appears serene beneath its gradually pitched roof. The residents enjoy great views through large expanses of glass.

LEFT Rustic detailing, including a barn-like door and floors of recycled antique oak, imbue the interior with character.

ABOVE The owners requested covered sitting porches on at lest two sides. Because the porches ran the risk of making the interior too dark, the decision was made to arrange the rooms around a high, skylit entry, surrounded by interior openings allowing light to pour into every room.

ABOVE In contrast to the impression created by the low, horizontal lines of the roof, the interior is tall and generous in feeling.

RIGHT Four huge pine columns give a temple-like quality to what is the cultural center of the home—an area containing an upright piano and a wall of bookshelves complete with a rolling ladder.

FOREST HOUSE

The traditional method of building in difficult terrain involves putting in a solid—and massive-looking—foundation, usually of stone or concrete. That technique usually proves effective from an engineering point of view, but in some locations, it draws too much attention to the house and to the imposing, sometimes bulky-looking base. What's often better is to use a lighter style of construction that will allow the house to appear as if it's floating above its site.

Peter Bohlin did that with the Forest house, which sits astride a hillside in West Cornwall, Connecticut. Concrete piers support the house while conveying the illusion of near-weightlessness. The industrial sash of the windows—simple and straightforward—brings the feeling of the woods inside. The way the exterior walls are pared away for a huge window assembly gives the house an abstract character that reduces the house's visual intrusion on nature. The intense color of the sash and of a few other elements provides just enough liveliness to make it clear that the house is not trying entirely to camouflage its presence. The drooping lamp over the beginning of the entrance ramp brings to mind a bright flower blooming in the moistness of the forest.

The house touches the land as little as possible, a good tactic when the objective is to make the landscape seem unconquered and pristine. The ultra-simple decks and entrance walkway, and the reduction of the roof to nothing more than a sharp angle, complete the remarkable effect.

LEFT Outdoors merges with indoors, thanks to the huge expanses of industrial sash, which wrap the corner.

ABOVE The house appears to float above the landscape on its concrete piers. The window area is such a continuous expanse of industrial sash that the house appears barely enclosed.

LEFT The floor and the window area step down together, creating good places for sitting and looking out.

ABOVE A wood bridge avoids stepping on the landscape.

LEFT *The green-stained house has such a simple shape that it doesn't compete with its setting for attention. The boardwalk-like decks reach into the woods.*

ABOVE *From a bedroom, the forest floor looks strangely beautiful, like the bottom of an ocean. Cantilevering and large areas of glass let the residents enjoy the setting to the utmost.*

PLATES

GAFFNEY RESIDENCE

PAGE 114

THIRD-FLOOR PLAN

K. Den/Bedroom

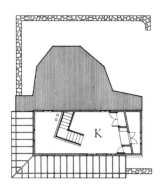

SECOND-FLOOR PLAN

H. Bedroom

I. Balcony

J. Closet

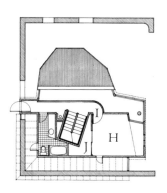

SOUTH ELEVATION

NORTH ELEVATION

FIRST-FLOOR PLAN

A. Courtyard

B. Entry

C. Kitchen

D. Dining Room

E. Living Room

F. Closet

G. Utility

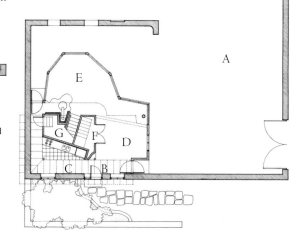

KAHN RESIDENCE

PAGE 120

SITE PLAN

SECOND-FLOOR PLAN

K. Bedroom

L. Bath

M. Master Bedroom

N. Master Bath

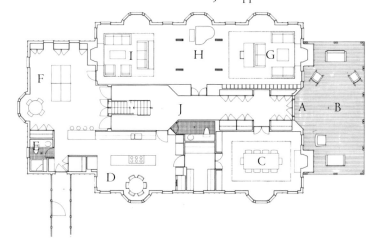

FIRST-FLOOR PLAN

A. Entry

B. Porch

C. Dining Room

D. Kitchen

E. Powder Room

F. Play Room

G. Living Room

H. Music Room

I. 2nd Living Room

J. Upper Hall

WINDHOVER

PAGE 126

SECOND-FLOOR PLAN

I.   Loft

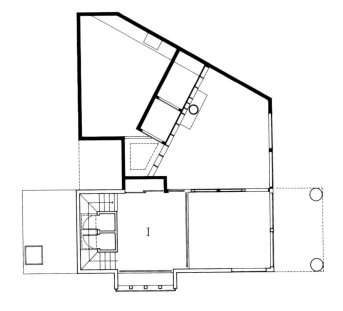

SITE PLAN

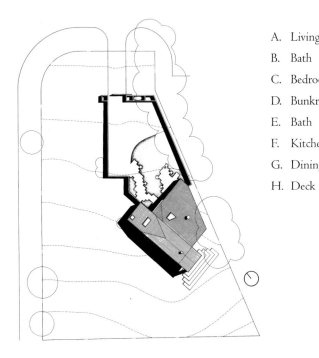

FIRST-FLOOR PLAN

A. Living Room

B. Bath

C. Bedroom

D. Bunkroom

E. Bath

F. Kitchen

G. Dining

H. Deck

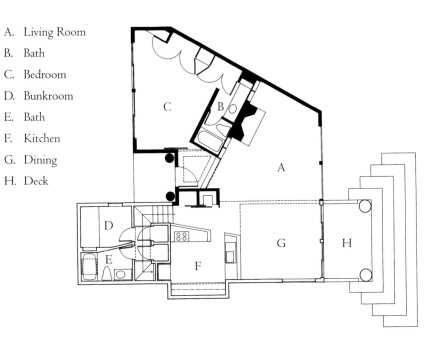

OLD MISSION COTTAGE

PAGE 132

SECOND-FLOOR PLAN

H. Master Bedroom

I. Walk-in Closet

J. Bedroom

K. Open to Below

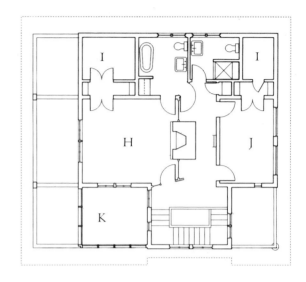

FIRST-FLOOR PLAN

A. Porch

B. Entry

C. Kitchen

D. Pantry

E. Dining Room

F. Living Room

G. Screened Porch

WEST ELEVATION

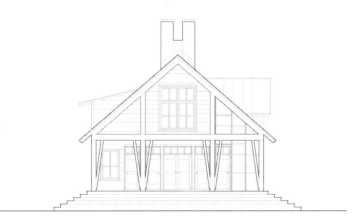

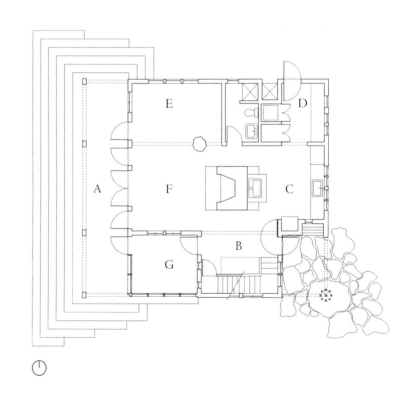

TUNIPUS COMPOUND

PAGE 140

SITE PLAN

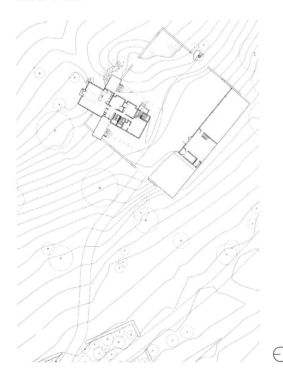

FLOOR PLAN

A. Front Deck
B. Entry
C. Living
D. Dining
E. Kitchen

F. Back Deck
G. Study
H. Bedroom
I. Master Bedroom
J. Outdoor Shower

K. Wetland
L. Office
M. Workshop
N. Storage Room
O. Driveway

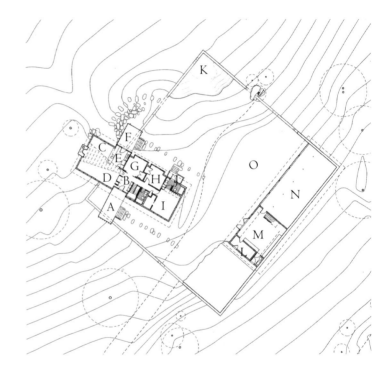

SOHN RESIDENCE

PAGE 148

FLOOR PLAN

A. Garage
B. Laundry
C. Dining Room
D. Living Room

E. Porch
F. Master Bedroom
G. Bedroom
H. Playroom

I. Guest Bedroom
J. Library
K. Kitchen

SITE PLAN

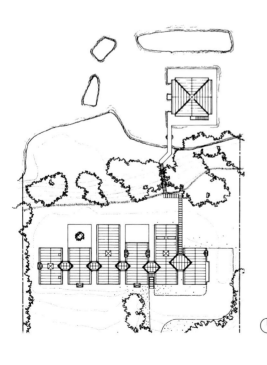

ELEVATION

TIN ROOF

PAGE 156

SITE PLAN

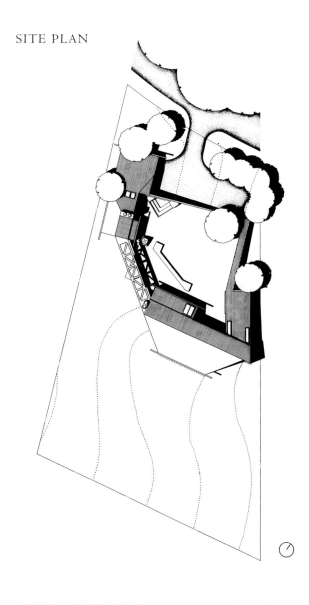

FLOOR PLAN

A. Courtyard

B. Garage

C. Stacked Guest Rooms

D. Living/Dining

E. Kitchen

F. Bedroom

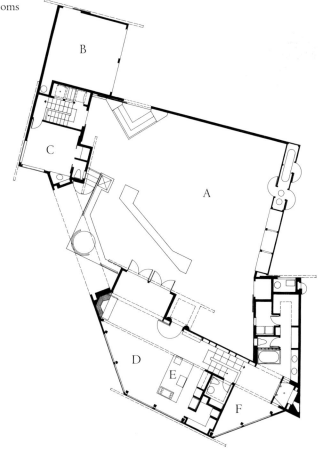

TOM & KARIN'S PLACE

PAGE 164

SITE PLAN

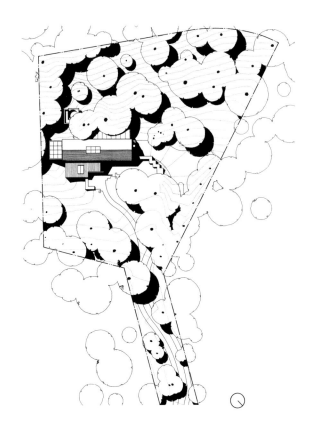

UPPER-LEVEL PLAN

K. Guest Bedroom

L. Loft

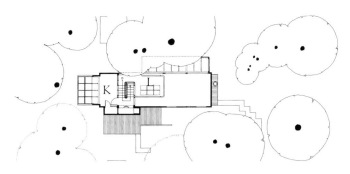

MAIN-LEVEL PLAN

B. Entry	F. Guest Bath	J. Spa
C. Living Room	G. Dining	
D. Terrace	H. Master Bath	
E. Kitchen	I. Master Bedroom	

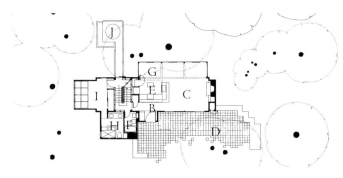

LOWER-LEVEL PLAN

A. Tandem Garage

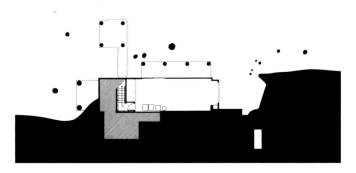

GREENE RESIDENCE

PAGE 170

SECOND-FLOOR PLAN

L. His Studio

M. Her Studio

N. Open

O. Guest Suite

P. Bath

Q. Staff Quarters

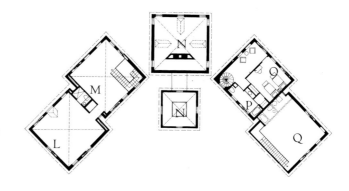

FIRST-FLOOR PLAN

A. Entry

B. Powder Room

C. Bath

D. Master Bedroom

E. Library

F. Living Room

G. Dining Room

H. Kitchen

I. Garage

J. Pool

K. Cabana

SITE PLAN

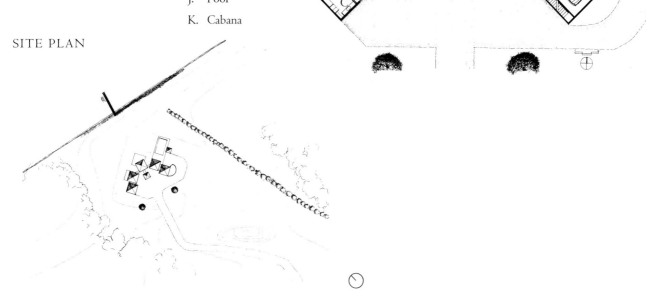

OREGON COAST HOUSE

PAGE 180

FLOOR PLAN

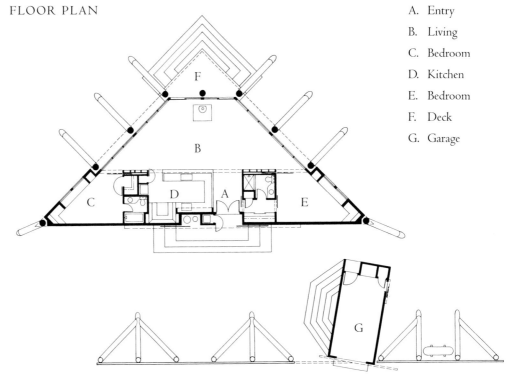

A. Entry
B. Living
C. Bedroom
D. Kitchen
E. Bedroom
F. Deck
G. Garage

SITE PLAN

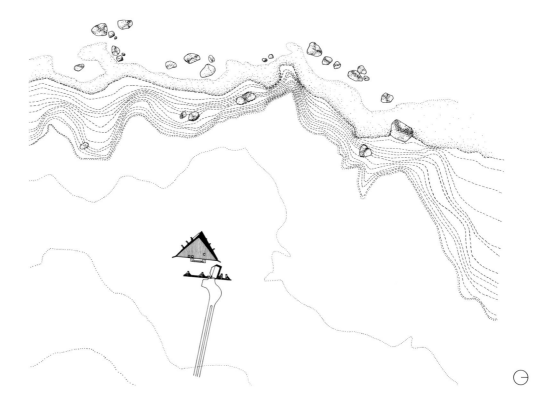

PALMEDO RESIDENCE

PAGE 188

SECOND-FLOOR PLAN

M. Roof

N. Open Boy

O. Bath

P. Study

Q. Open

R. Stair

S. Link Entry

T. Open Above

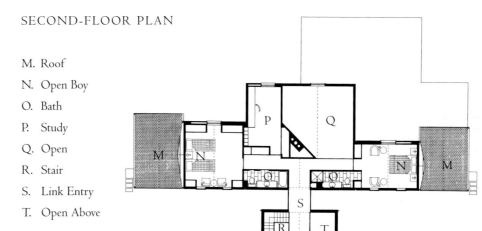

FIRST-FLOOR PLAN

A. Entry

B. Stair

C. Open Above

D. Master Bedroom

E. Master Bath

F. Powder Room

G. Gallery

H. Library

I. Living Room

J. Entrance Hall

K. Dining Room

L. Kitchen

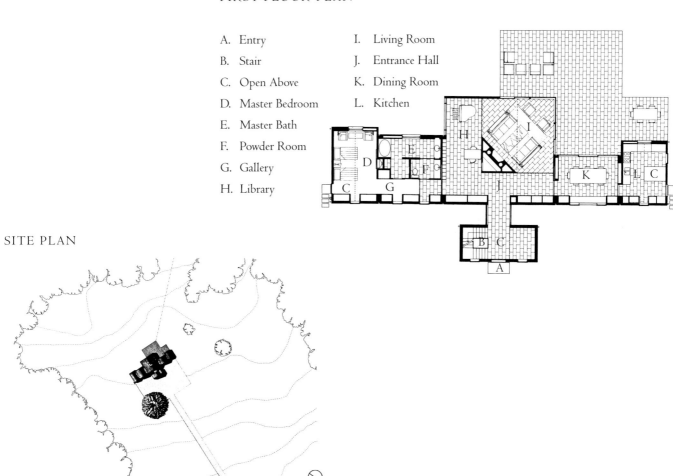

SITE PLAN

GEORGIAN BAY RETREAT

PAGE 196

SECOND-FLOOR PLAN

I.   Bedroom

J.   Recreation

K. Sauna

L.   Utility

FIRST-FLOOR PLAN

A. Deck

B. Entry

C. Kitchen

D. Dining Room

E. Living Room

F. Fireplace Sitting

G. Master Bedroom

H. Bedroom

NORTH ELEVATION

SOUTH ELEVATION

MCKINNEY HOUSE

PAGE 204

FIRST-FLOOR PLAN

I. Dressing Room

J. Master Bedroom

K. Living Room

L. Bath

M. Kitchen

N. Dining Room

O. Breakfast Room

P. Studio

Q. Guest Bedroom

R. Guest Bath

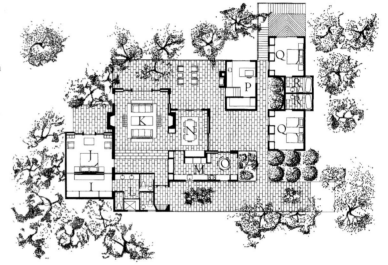

LOWER-LEVEL PLAN

A. Covered Area

B. Cabana

C. Sauna

D. Mechanical

E. Play Room

F. Guest Bedroom

G. Guest Bath

H. Open

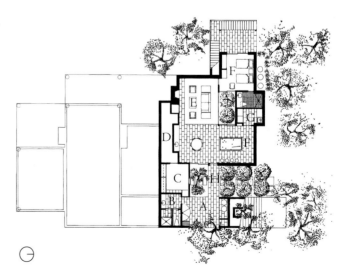

PINS SUR MER

PAGE 210

FLOOR PLAN

A. Entry
B. Entry Porch
C. Bath
D. Bedroom
E. Kitchen
F. Dining
G. Living
H. Bath
I. Bedroom
J. Porch

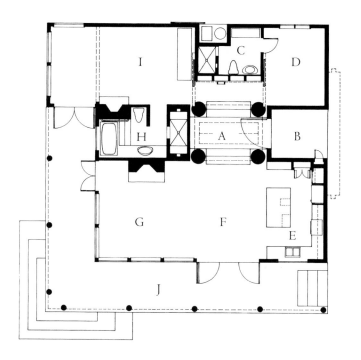

SITE PLAN

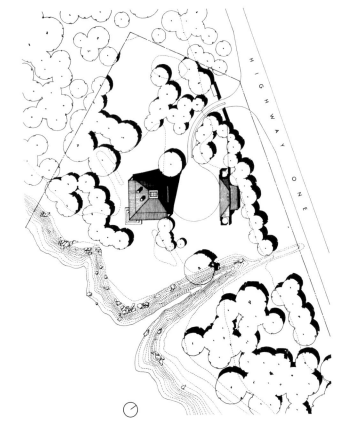

FOREST HOUSE

PAGE 216

SECOND-FLOOR PLAN

F. Open to Below

G. Study

H. Storage

I. Guest Bedroom

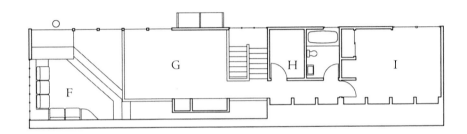

FIRST-FLOOR PLAN

A. Living Room

B. Dining Room

C. Kitchen

D. Utility

E. Master Bedroom

CREDITS

Front Cover: Tom Rider

Introduction Photography:

Jeff Goldberg/Esto. Page 8

12, Michael Freeman from *Barn: The Art of Working Building* by David Larkin, Elric Endersby and Alexander Greenwood. Compilation copyright © 1982 by David Larkin. Reproduced by permission of Houghton Mifflin Company. All rights reserved. Page 12

Richard Neutra VDL Research House. Page 13

Mimi Sloane, owner of the copyrights in the works of Eric Sloane. Page 14

Courtesy of the Adirondack Museum. Page 15

George M. Cushing Jr. and the Boston Athenaeum. Page 16

Charles Sumner Greene Collection (1959–I) Environmental Design Archives, University of California, Berkeley. Page 17

Shaker Village of Pleasant Hill, Kentucky. Page 18

Shaker Museum at South Union, Kentucky. Page 19

Peter Aaron/Esto. Page 19 (bottom)

Bohlin Cywinski Jackson:

Michael Awad. Pages 6/7, 12 (bottom), 54, 62/63, 92, 196, 197, 198/199, 200, 201, 202, 203

Karl Backus. Pages 22, 44/45, 48, 51, 58, 64, 72, 86, 96, 98, 105, 108, 111, 134, 135, 136

Dan Bibb. Pages 52, 68, 78, 102, 104, 132, 133, 137

Joseph Molitor, Courtesy of Avery Architectural and Fine Arts Library, Columbia University in the City of New York. Pages 114, 116, 117, 118, 119

Sandy Nixon Taylor (c/o Architectural Archives of Columbia University). Page 115

Michael Thomas. Pages 2/3, 24/25, 28, 34, 35, 37, 42, 46, 47 (bottom), 56, 59, 80, 83, 84 (top), 84 (bottom), 89, 103 (bottom), 106, 140, 141, 142, 143, 144/145, 146, 147, 216, 217, 218, 219, 220, 221

Hugh Newell Jacobsen:

Robert Lautman. Pages 11 (bottom), 15 (top), 18 (top), 26 (top), 26 (bottom), 29, 30/31, 33, 39, 40, 41, 47 (top), 49, 61, 65, 75, 76, 81, 82 (top, middle, bottom), 87 (top), 87 (bottom), 97, 100, 120, 121, 122, 123, 124/125, 148, 149, 150, 151, 152, 153, 154, 155, 170, 171, 172, 173, 174, 175, 176, 177, 188, 189, 190, 191, 192, 193, 194, 195, 204, 205, 206, 207, 208, 209 (top), 209 (bottom)

Obie G. Bowman Architect, AIA:

Obie G. Bowman. Pages 14 (top), 43, 69, 70/71, 73, 77, 79, 85, 90, 94, 99, 101 (bottom), 103 (top), 107, 109, 158, 159, 163, 164, 165, 168, 169

Erhard Pfeiffer. Pages 16 (top), 156, 157, 160, 161, 162

Tom Rider. Pages 13 (top), 17 (top), 23, 27, 32, 36, 38, 50, 53, 55, 57 (top), 57 (bottom), 60, 74, 88, 93, 95, 101(top), 110, 126, 127, 128, 129, 130/131, 180, 181, 182, 183, 184, 185, 186, 187, 210, 211, 212, 213, 214, 215

Richard Sexton. Pages 166, 167

Back Cover :

Robert Lautman

Flap Portrait:

Lush Photography & Design Inc. © 2001

Illustration Credits:

Peter Bohlin. Page 1

Fort Klock Historical Society. Page 9

C. Fraser from *A Field Guide to American Architecture* by Carole Rifkind. Page 10

(Fig. 128. Cottage-Villa in the Rural Gothic Style) appearing on page 296 of *Architecture of Country Houses* by A.J. Downing. Page 11

Hugh Newell Jacobsen. Page 20

Peter Bohlin. Page 66

Obie G. Bowman. Page 112

Peter Bohlin. Page 138